Canoeing in the
Wilderness

Canoeing in the Wilderness

Henry David Thoreau

This edition published in 2020 by Arcturus Publishing Limited
26/27 Bickels Yard, 151–153 Bermondsey Street,
London SE1 3HA

AD007617US

Printed in the UK

❀ CONTENTS ❀

INTRODUCTION

HENRY DAVID THOREAU was born in 1817 in Concord, Massachusetts. With the help of his older siblings, John Jr. and Helen, who contributed portions of their teaching salaries to pay his tuition expenses, he was able to attend Harvard University. After graduating in 1837, Henry went on to become a teacher at the Concord public school. It was only two weeks later that he resigned when he found himself in a dispute with the superintendent of the school on the proper way to discipline children.

In 1838, Henry and his brother, John Jr., opened their own school together. He worked there until John Jr. fell ill in 1841.

While renting a room in his parents' home, Henry was invited to work as a live-in handyman by his friend and neighbor, Ralph Waldo Emerson. By this time, Emerson was a successful author and philosopher, well-known for his theories on transcendentalism. In April 1841, Thoreau moved into the Emerson household. During his two-year stay there, Henry was encouraged to develop his literary talents, and with Emerson's help, he soon managed to get several poems and essays published in the journal, *The Dial*.

When he returned to Concord, he was reminded of the drudgeries of life. His days were occupied with tedious work in the Thoreau pencil factory, and at home he had little privacy or quiet, as his mother often took in boarders.

So Thoreau took matters into his own hands. In 1845, he set to work building a cabin on a small part of Emerson's land by Walden Pond. It was to be his sanctuary, where he could live peacefully and focus on the life of the mind. Henry moved into his new abode in early July. There, he turned traditional American values on their head by choosing to work one day a week while resting for six. For two years he lived this way. His most famous book, *Walden* (1854), began as a written lecture in response to the many questions Thoreau received from family, friends and locals about his new way of life.

Three years later he made a trip through the forests of Maine. The region had escaped the rapid development and industrialization that marked much of the United States during this period and it remained sparsely populated, with only the occasional logger, farmer, or Native American to disturb the tranquillity of nature. He recorded his travels in *The Maine Woods* (1864), the latter half of which was to be split into a separate book, *Canoeing in the Wilderness*. Thoreau's love for the wilderness shines through his writing and demonstrates an unbridled enthusiasm for the natural world.

Thoreau continued to travel, visiting the Great Lakes in 1861, and he devoured the accounts of the great explorers of the era, including those of Lewis and Clark, John Franklin, David Livingstone, and many others. After John Brown's raid on Harper's Ferry in 1859, Thoreau issued a powerful defense of Brown's actions. During the 1860s, his health steadily declined, and he died in 1862.

❧ CHAPTER I ❧

Monday, Tuesday, Wednesday, Thursday
July 20–23, 1857

I STARTED ON my third excursion to the Maine woods Monday, July 20, 1857, with one companion, arriving at Bangor the next day at noon. The succeeding morning, a relative of mine who is well acquainted with the Penobscot Indians took me in his wagon to Oldtown to assist me in obtaining an Indian for this expedition. We were ferried across to the Indian Island in a bateau. The ferryman's boy had the key to it, but the father, who was a blacksmith, after a little hesitation, cut the chain with a cold chisel on the rock. He told me that the Indians were nearly all gone to the seaboard and to Massachusetts, partly on account of the smallpox, of which they are very much afraid, having broken out in Oldtown. The old chief Neptune, however, was there still.

The first man we saw on the island was an Indian named Joseph Polis, whom my relative addressed familiarly as "Joe." He was dressing a deerskin in his yard. The skin was spread over a slanting log, and he was scraping it with a stick held by both hands. He was stoutly built, perhaps a little above the middle height, with a broad face, and, as others said, perfect Indian features and complexion. His house was a two-story white one with blinds, the best-looking that I noticed there, and as good as an average one on a New England village street. It was surrounded by a garden and fruit trees, single cornstalks standing thinly amid the beans. We asked him if he knew any good Indian who would like to go into the woods with us, that is, to the Allegash Lakes by way of Moosehead, and return by the East Branch of the Penobscot.

To which he answered out of that strange remoteness in which the Indian ever dwells to the white man, "Me like to go myself; me want to get some moose"; and kept on scraping the skin.

The ferryman had told us that all the best Indians were gone except Polis, who was one of the aristocracy. He, to be sure, would be the best man we could have, but if he went at all would want a great price. Polis asked at first two dollars a day but agreed to go for a dollar and a half, and fifty cents a week for his canoe. He would come to Bangor with his canoe by the seven o'clock train that evening—we might depend on him. We thought ourselves lucky to secure the services of this man, who was known to be particularly steady and trustworthy.

I spent the afternoon with my companion, who had remained in Bangor, in preparing for our expedition, purchasing provisions, hard-bread,★ pork, coffee, sugar, etc., and some india-rubber clothing.

At evening the Indian arrived in the cars, and I led the way, while he followed me, three quarters of a mile to my friend's house, with the canoe on his head. I did not know the exact route, but steered by the lay of the land, as I do in Boston. I tried to enter into conversation with

---

★ Hard-bread or ship-bread is a kind of hard biscuit commonly baked in large cakes and much used by sailors and soldiers.

him, but as he was puffing under the weight of his canoe, not having the usual apparatus for carrying it, but, above all, as he was an Indian, I might as well have been thumping on the bottom of his birch the while. In answer to the various observations that I made he only grunted vaguely from beneath his canoe once or twice, so that I knew he was there.

Early the next morning the stage called for us. My companion and I had each a large knapsack as full as it would hold, and we had two large rubber bags which held our provisions and utensils. As for the Indian, all the baggage he had, beside his axe and gun, was a blanket, which he brought loose in his hand. However, he had laid in a store of tobacco and a new pipe for the excursion. The canoe was securely lashed diagonally across the top of the stage, with bits of carpet tucked under the edge to prevent its chafing. The driver appeared as much accustomed to carrying canoes in this way as bandboxes.

At the Bangor House we took in four men bound on a hunting excursion, one of the men going as cook. They had a dog, a middling-sized brindled cur, which ran by the side of the stage, his master showing his head and whistling from time to time. But after we had gone about three miles the dog was suddenly missing, and two of the party went back for him, while the stage, which was full of passengers, waited. At length one man came back, while the other kept on. This whole party of hunters declared their intention to stop till the dog was found, but the very obliging driver was ready to wait a spell longer. He was evidently unwilling to lose so many passengers, who would have taken a private conveyance, or perhaps the other line of stages, the next day. Such progress did we make, with a journey of over sixty miles to be accomplished that day, and a rainstorm just setting in. We discussed the subject of dogs and their instincts till it was threadbare, while we waited there, and the scenery of the suburbs of Bangor is still distinctly impressed on my memory.

After full half an hour the man returned, leading the dog by a rope. He had overtaken him just as he was entering the Bangor House. He was then tied on the top of the stage, but, being wet and cold, several times in the course of the journey he jumped off, and I saw him dangling by his neck. This dog was depended on to stop bears. He had already stopped one somewhere in New Hampshire, and I can testify that he stopped a stage in Maine. This party of four probably paid nothing for the dog's ride, nor for his run, while our party of three paid two dollars—and were charged four—for the light canoe which lay still on the top.

The stage was crowded all the way. If you had looked inside you would have thought that we were prepared to run the gantlet of a band of robbers, for there were four or five guns on the front seat and one or two on the back one, each man holding his darling in his arms. It appeared that this party of hunters was going our way, but much farther. Their leader was a handsome man about thirty years old, of good height, but not apparently robust, of gentlemanly address and faultless toilet. He had a fair white complexion as if he had always lived in the shade, and an intellectual face, and with his quiet manners might have passed for a divinity student who had seen something of the world. I was surprised to find that he was probably the chief white hunter of Maine and was known all along the road. I afterwards heard him spoken of as one who could endure a great deal of exposure and fatigue without showing the effect of it; and he could not only use guns, but make them, being himself a gunsmith. In the spring he had saved a stage-driver and two passengers from drowning in the backwater of the Piscataquis on this road, having swum ashore in the freezing water and made a raft and got them off—though the horses were drowned—at great risk to himself, while the only other man who could swim withdrew to the nearest house to prevent freezing. He knew our man, and remarked that we had a good Indian there, a good hunter; adding that he was said to be worth six thousand dollars. The Indian also knew him, and said to me, "The great hunter."

The Indian sat on the front seat with a stolid expression of face as if barely awake to what was going on. Again I was struck by the peculiar vagueness of his replies when addressed in the stage or at the taverns. He really never said anything on such occasions. He was merely stirred up like a wild beast, and passively muttered some insignificant response. His answer, in such cases, was vague as a puff of smoke, suggesting no *responsibility*, and if you considered it you would find that you had got nothing out of him. This was instead of the conventional palaver and smartness of the white man, and equally profitable. Most get no more than this out of the Indian, and pronounce him stolid accordingly. I was surprised to see what a foolish and impertinent style a Maine man, a passenger, used in addressing him, as if he were a child, which only made his eyes glisten a little. A tipsy Canadian asked him at a tavern, in a drawling tone, if he smoked, to which he answered with an indefinite "Yes."

"Won't you lend me your pipe a little while?" asked the other.

He replied, looking straight by the man's head, with a face singularly vacant to all neighboring interests, "Me got no pipe"; yet I had seen him put a new one, with a supply of tobacco, into his pocket that morning.

Our little canoe, so neat and strong, drew a favorable criticism from all the wiseacres among the tavern loungers along the road. By the roadside, close to the wheels, I noticed a splendid great purple fringed orchis which I would fain have stopped the stage to pluck, but as this had never been known to stop a bear, like the cur on the stage, the driver would probably have thought it a waste of time.

When we reached the lake, about half past eight in the evening, it was still steadily raining, and in that fresh, cool atmosphere the hylas were peeping and the toads ringing about the lake. It was as if the season had revolved backward two or three months, or I had arrived at the abode of perpetual spring.

We had expected to go upon the lake at once, and, after paddling up two or three miles, to camp on one of its islands, but on account of the rain we decided to go to one of the taverns for the night.

⸙ CHAPTER II ⸙

Friday, July 24

ABOUT FOUR O'CLOCK the next morning, though it was quite cloudy, accompanied by the landlord to the water's edge, in the twilight, we launched our canoe from a rock on Moosehead Lake. We had a rather small canoe for three persons, eighteen and one fourth feet long by two feet six and one half inches wide in the middle, and one foot deep within. I judged that it would weigh not far from eighty pounds. The Indian had recently made it himself, and its smallness was partly compensated for by its newness, as well as stanchness and solidity, it being made of very thick bark and ribs. Our baggage weighed about one hundred and sixty-six pounds. The principal part of the baggage was, as usual, placed in the middle of the broadest part, while we stowed ourselves in the chinks and crannies that were left before and behind it, where there was no room to extend our legs, the loose articles being tucked into the ends. The canoe was thus as closely packed as a market basket. The Indian sat on a crossbar in the stern, but we flat on the bottom with a splint or chip behind our backs to protect them from the crossbar, and one of us commonly paddled with the Indian.

Paddling along the eastern side of the lake in the still of the morning, we soon saw a few sheldrakes, which the Indian called *Shecorways*, and some peetweets on the rocky shore. We also saw and heard loons. It was inspiriting to hear the regular dip of the paddles, as if they were our fins or flippers, and to realize that we were at length fairly embarked.

Having passed the small rocky isles within two or three miles of the foot of the lake, we had a short consultation respecting our course, and inclined to the western shore for the sake of its lee; for otherwise, if the wind should rise, it would be impossible for us to reach Mount Kineo, which is about midway up the lake on the east side, but at its narrowest part, where probably we could recross if we took the western side. The wind is the chief obstacle to crossing the lakes, especially in so small a canoe. The Indian remarked several times that he did not like to cross the lakes "in littlum canoe," but nevertheless, "just as we say, it made no odds to him."

Moosehead Lake is twelve miles wide at the widest place, and thirty miles long in a direct line, but longer as it lies. Paddling near the shore, we frequently heard the *pe-pe* of the olive-sided flycatcher, also the wood pewee and the kingfisher. The Indian reminding us that he could not work without eating, we stopped to breakfast on the main shore southwest of Deer Island. We took out our bags, and the Indian made a fire under a very large bleached log, using white pine bark from a stump, though he said that hemlock was better, and kindling with canoe birch bark. Our table was a large piece of freshly peeled birch bark, laid wrong side up, and our breakfast consisted of hard-bread, fried pork, and strong coffee well sweetened, in which we did not miss the milk.

While we were getting breakfast a brood of twelve black dippers★, half grown, came paddling by within three or four rods, not at all alarmed; and they loitered about as long as we stayed, now huddled close together, now moving off in a long line, very cunningly.

Looking northward from this place it appeared as if we were entering a large bay, and we did not know whether we should be obliged to diverge from our course and keep outside a point which we saw, or should find a passage between this and the mainland. It was misty dog-day weather, and we had already penetrated a smaller bay of the same kind, and knocked the bottom out of it, though we had been obliged to pass over a bar between an island and the shore, where there was but just breadth and depth enough to float the canoe, and the Indian had observed, "Very easy makum bridge here," but now it seemed that if we held on we should be fairly embayed. Presently, however, the mist lifted somewhat and revealed a break in the shore northward. The Indian immediately remarked, "I guess you and I go there."

This was his common expression instead of saying "we." He never addressed us by our names, though curious to know how they were spelled and what they meant. We called him Polis. He had already guessed very accurately at our ages, and said that he was forty-eight.

After breakfast I emptied the melted pork that was left into the lake, making what the sailors call a "slick," and watching to see how much it spread over and smoothed

---

★ The name dipper is applied to several species of water-birds that are notable for their skill in diving.

the agitated surface. The Indian looked at it a moment and said, "That make hard paddlum through; hold 'em canoe. So say old times."

We hastily reloaded, putting the dishes loose in the bows, that they might be at hand when wanted, and set out again. The western shore, near which we paddled along, rose gently to a considerable height and was everywhere densely covered with the forest, in which was a large proportion of hard wood to enliven and relieve the fir and spruce.

The Indian said that the lichen which we saw hanging from the trees was called *chorchorque*. We asked him the names of several birds which we heard this morning. The thrush, which was quite common, and whose note he imitated, he said was called *Adelungquamooktum*; but sometimes he could not tell the name of some small bird which I heard and knew, but he said, "I tell all the birds about here; can't tell littlum noise, but I see 'em, then I can tell."

I observed that I should like to go to school to him to learn his language, living on the Indian island the while; could not that be done?

"Oh, yer," he replied, "good many do so."

I asked how long he thought it would take. He said one week. I told him that in this voyage I would tell him all I knew, and he should tell me all he knew, to which he readily agreed.

Mount Kineo, which was generally visible, though occasionally concealed by islands or the mainland in front, had a level bar of cloud concealing its summit, and all the mountain-tops about the lake were cut off at the same height. Ducks of various kinds were quite common, and ran over the water before us as fast as a horse trots.

The Indian asked the meaning of *reality*, as near as I could make out the word, which he said one of us had used; also of *interrent*, that is, intelligent. I observed that he could rarely sound the letter r, but used l, as also r for l sometimes; as *load* for road, *pickelel* for pickerel, *Soogle* Island for Sugar Island. He generally added the syllable *um* to his words, as *paddlum*, etc.

On a point on the mainland where we landed to stretch our legs and look at the vegetation, going inland a few steps, I discovered a fire still glowing beneath its ashes, where somebody had breakfasted, and a bed of twigs prepared for the following night. So I knew not only that they had just left, but that they designed to return, and by the breadth of the bed that there was more than one in the party. You might have gone within six feet of these signs without seeing them. There grew the beaked hazel, rue seven feet high, and red osier, whose bark the Indian said was good to smoke, "tobacco before white people came to this country, Indian tobacco."

The Indian was always very careful in approaching the shore, lest he should injure his canoe on the rocks, letting it swing round slowly sidewise, and was still more particular that we should not step into it on shore, nor till it floated free, and then should step gently lest we should open its seams, or make a hole in the bottom.

After passing Deer Island we saw the little steamer from Greenville, far east in the middle of the lake. Sometimes we could hardly tell her from an island which had a few trees on it. Here we were exposed to the wind from over the whole breadth of the lake, and ran a little risk of being swamped. While I had my eye fixed on the spot where a large fish had leaped, we took in a gallon or two of water; but we soon reached the shore and took the canoe over the bar at Sand-bar Island, a few feet wide only, and so saved a considerable distance.

We crossed a broad bay and found the water quite rough. A very little wind on these broad lakes raises a sea which will swamp a canoe. Looking off from the shore, the surface may appear to be almost smooth a mile distant, or if you see a few white crests they appear nearly level with the rest of the lake, but when you get out so far, you may find quite a sea running, and ere long, before you think of it, a wave will gently creep up the side of the canoe and fill your lap, like a monster deliberately covering you with its slime before it swallows you, or it will strike the canoe violently and break into it. The same thing may happen when the wind rises suddenly, though it were perfectly calm and smooth there a few minutes before; so that nothing can save you, unless you can swim ashore, for it is impossible to get into a canoe when it is upset. Since you sit flat on the bottom, though the danger should not be imminent, a little water is a great inconvenience, not to mention the wetting of your provisions. We rarely crossed even a bay directly, from point to point, when there was wind, but made a slight curve corresponding somewhat to the shore, that we might the sooner reach it if the wind increased.

When the wind is aft, and not too strong, the Indian makes a spritsail of his blanket. He thus easily skims over the whole length of this lake in a day.

The Indian paddled on one side, and one of us on the other, to keep the canoe steady, and when he wanted to change hands he would say, "T' other side." He asserted, in answer to our questions, that he had never upset a canoe himself, though he may have been upset by others.

Think of our little eggshell of a canoe tossing across that great lake, a mere black speck to the eagle soaring above it!

My companion trailed for trout as we paddled along, but, the Indian warning him that a big fish might upset us, for there are some very large ones there, he agreed to pass the line quickly to the stern if he had a bite.

While we were crossing this bay, where Mount Kineo rose dark before us within two or three miles, the Indian repeated the tradition respecting this mountain's having anciently been a cow moose—how a mighty Indian hunter succeeded in killing this queen of the moose tribe with great difficulty, while her calf was killed somewhere among the islands in Penobscot Bay, and, to his eyes, this mountain had still the form of the moose in a reclining posture. He told this at some length and with apparent good faith, and asked us how we supposed the hunter could have killed such a mighty moose as that. An Indian tells such a story as if he thought it deserved to have a good deal said about it, only he has not got it to say, and so he makes up for the deficiency by a drawling tone, long-windedness, and a dumb wonder which he hopes will be contagious.

We approached the land again through pretty rough water, and then steered directly across the lake at its narrowest part to the eastern side, and were soon partly under the lee of the mountain, having paddled about twenty miles. It was now about noon.

We designed to stop there that afternoon and night, and spent half an hour looking along the shore northward for a suitable place to camp. At length, by going half a dozen rods into the dense spruce and fir wood on the side of the mountain almost as dark as a cellar, we found a place sufficiently clear and level to lie down on, after cutting away a few bushes. The Indian cleared a path to it from the shore with his axe, and we then carried up all our baggage, pitched our tent, and made our bed, in order to be ready for foul weather, which then threatened us, and for the night. He gathered a large armful of fir twigs, breaking them off, which he said were the best for our bed, partly, I thought, because they were the largest and could be most rapidly collected. It had been raining more or less for four or five days, and the wood was even damper than usual, but he got dry bark from the under side of a dead leaning hemlock, which he said he could always do.

This noon his mind was occupied with a law question, and I referred him to my companion, who was a lawyer. It appeared that he had been buying land lately—I think it was a hundred acres—but there was probably an incumbrance to it, somebody else claiming to have bought some grass on it for this year. He wished to know to whom the grass belonged, and was told that if the other man could prove that he bought the grass before he, Polis, bought the land, the former could take it whether the latter knew it or not. To which he only answered, "Strange!" He went over this several times, fairly sat down to it, with his back to a tree, as if he meant to confine us to this topic henceforth; but as he made no headway, only reached the jumping-off place of his wonder at white men's institutions after each explanation, we let the subject die.

He said that he had fifty acres of grass, potatoes, etc., somewhere above Oldtown, besides some about his house; that he hired a good deal of his work, hoeing, etc., and preferred white men to Indians because "they keep steady and know how."

After dinner we returned southward along the shore, in the canoe, on account of the difficulty of climbing over the rocks and fallen trees, and began to ascend the mountain along the edge of the precipice. But, a smart shower coming up just then, the Indian crept under his canoe, while we, protected by our rubber coats, proceeded to botanize. So we sent him back to the camp for shelter, agreeing that he should come for us with his canoe toward night. It had rained a little in the forenoon, and we trusted that this would be the clearing-up shower, which it proved; but our feet and legs were thoroughly wet by the bushes. The clouds breaking away a little, we had a glorious wild view, as we ascended, of the broad lake with its numerous forest-clad islands extending beyond our sight both north and south, and the boundless forest undulating away from its shores on every side, as densely packed as a rye-field and enveloping nameless mountains in succession. It was a perfect lake of the woods.

Looking southward, the heavens were completely overcast, the mountains capped with clouds, and the lake generally wore a dark and stormy appearance, but from its surface six or eight miles distant there was reflected upward through the misty air a bright blue tinge from the unseen sky of another latitude beyond. They probably had a clear sky then at the south end of the lake.

Again we mistook a little rocky islet seen through the "drisk," with some taller bare trunks or stumps on it, for the steamer with its smoke-pipes, but as it had not changed its position after half an hour we were undeceived. So much do the works of man resemble the works of nature. A moose might mistake a steamer for a floating isle, and not be scared till he heard its puffing or its whistle.

If I wished to see a mountain or other scenery under the most favorable auspices, I would go to it in foul weather so as to be there when it cleared up. We are then in the most suitable mood, and nature is most fresh and inspiring. There is no serenity so fair as that which is just established in a tearful eye.

Jackson, in his "Report on the Geology of Maine," says: "Hornstone, which will answer for flints, occurs in various parts of the State. The largest mass of this stone known in the world is Mount Kineo, upon Moosehead Lake, which appears to be entirely composed of it, and rises seven hundred feet above the lake level. This variety of hornstone I have seen in every part of New England in the form of Indian arrow-heads, hatchets, chisels, etc., which were probably obtained from this mountain by the aboriginal inhabitants of the country."

I have myself found hundreds of arrow-heads made of the same material. It is generally slate-colored, with white specks, becoming a uniform white where exposed to the light and air. I picked up a small thin piece which had so sharp an edge that I used it as a knife, and, to see what I could do, fairly cut off an aspen one inch thick with it, by bending it and making many cuts; though I cut my fingers badly with the back of it in the meanwhile.

From the summit of the precipice which forms the southern and eastern sides of this mountain peninsula, five or six hundred feet high, we probably might have jumped down to the water, or to the seemingly dwarfish trees on the narrow neck of land which connects it with the main. It is a dangerous place to try the steadiness of your nerves.

The plants which attracted our attention on this mountain were the mountain cinquefoil, abundant and in bloom still at the very base by the waterside, very beautiful harebells overhanging the precipice, bearberry, the Canada blueberry, wild holly, the great round-leafed orchis, bunchberry, reddening as we ascended, green at the base of the mountain, red at the top, and the small fern *Woodsia ilvensis*, growing in tufts, now in fruit. Having explored the wonders of the mountain, and the weather being now cleared up, we commenced the descent. We met the Indian, puffing and panting, about one third of the way up, but thinking that he must be near the top. On reaching the canoe we found that he had caught a lake trout weighing about three pounds, while we were on the mountain.

When we got to the camp, the canoe was taken out and turned over, and a log laid across it to prevent its being blown away. The Indian cut some large logs of damp and rotten wood to smoulder and keep fire through the night. The trout was fried for supper.

Our tent was of thin cotton cloth and quite small, forming with the ground a triangular prism closed at the rear end, six feet long, seven wide, and four high, so that we could barely sit up in the middle. It required two forked stakes, a smooth ridgepole, and a dozen or more pins to pitch it. It kept off dew and wind and an ordinary rain, and answered our purpose well enough. We reclined within it till bedtime, each with his baggage at his head, or else sat about the fire, having hung our wet clothes on a pole before the fire for the night.

As we sat there, just before night, looking out through the dusky wood, the Indian heard a noise which he said was made by a snake. He imitated it at my request, making a low whistling note—*pheet*—*pheet*—two or three times repeated, somewhat like the peep of the hyla, but not so loud. He said that he had never seen them while making it, but going to the spot he finds the snake. This, he said, was a sign of rain. When I had selected this place for our camp he had remarked that there were snakes there. "But they won't do any hurt," I said.

"Oh, no," he answered, "just as you say; it makes no difference to me."

He lay on the right side of the tent, because, as he said, he was partly deaf in one ear, and he wanted to lie with his good ear up. As we lay there he inquired if I ever heard "Indian sing." I replied that I had not often, and asked him if he would not favor us with a song. He readily assented, and, lying on his back, with his blanket wrapped around him, he commenced a slow, somewhat nasal, yet musical chant, in his own language, which probably was taught his tribe long ago by the Catholic missionaries. He translated it to us, sentence by sentence, afterward. It proved to be a very simple religious exercise or hymn, the burden of which was that there was only one God who ruled all the world.

His singing carried me back to the period of the discovery of America, when Europeans first encountered the simple faith of the Indian. There was, indeed, a beautiful simplicity about it; nothing of the dark and savage, only the mild and infantile. The sentiments of humility and reverence chiefly were expressed.

It was a dense and damp spruce and fir wood in which we lay, and, except for our fire, perfectly dark; and when I awoke in the night, I either heard an owl from deeper in the forest behind us, or a loon from a distance over the lake. Getting up some time after midnight to collect the scattered brands together, while my companions were sound asleep, I observed, partly in the fire, which had ceased to blaze, a perfectly regular elliptical ring of light, about five inches in its shortest diameter, six or seven in its longer, and from one eighth to one quarter of an inch wide. It was fully as bright as the fire, but not reddish or scarlet like a coal, but a white and slumbering light, like the glowworm's. I saw at once that it must be phosphorescent wood, which I had often heard of, but never chanced to see. Putting my finger on it, with a little hesitation, I found that it was a piece of dead moosewood which the Indian had cut off in a slanting direction the evening before.

Using my knife, I discovered that the light proceeded from that portion of the sapwood immediately under the bark, and thus presented a regular ring at the end, and when I pared off the bark and cut into the sap, it was all aglow along the log. I was surprised to find the wood quite hard and apparently sound, though probably decay had commenced in the sap, and I cut out some little triangular chips, and, placing them in the hollow of my hand, carried them into the camp, waked my companion, and showed them to him. They lit up the inside of my hand, revealing the lines and wrinkles, and appearing exactly like coals of fire raised to a white heat.

I noticed that part of a decayed stump within four or five feet of the fire, an inch wide and six inches long, soft and shaking wood, shone with equal brightness.

I neglected to ascertain whether our fire had anything to do with this, but the previous day's rain and long-continued wet weather undoubtedly had.

I was exceedingly interested by this phenomenon. It could hardly have thrilled me more if it had taken the form of letters, or of the human face. I little thought that there was such a light shining in the darkness of the wilderness for me.

The next day the Indian told me their name for the light—*artoosoqu'*—and on my inquiring concerning the will-o'-the-wisp he said that his "folks" sometimes saw fires passing along at various heights, even as high as the trees, and making a noise. I was prepared after this to hear of the most startling and unimagined phenomena witnessed by "his folks," they are abroad at all hours and seasons in scenes so unfrequented by white men. Nature must have made a thousand revelations to them which are still secrets to us.

I did not regret my not having seen this before, since I now saw it under circumstances so favorable. I was in just the frame of mind to see something wonderful, and this was a phenomenon adequate to my circumstances and expectation, and it put me on the alert to see more like it. I let science slide, and rejoiced in that light as if it had been a fellow creature. A scientific *explanation*, as it is called, would have been altogether out of place there. That is for pale daylight. Science with its retorts would have put me to sleep; it was the opportunity to be ignorant that I improved. It made a believer of me more than before. I believed that the woods were not tenantless, but choke-full of honest spirits as good as myself any day—not an empty chamber in which chemistry was left to work alone, but an inhabited house. It suggested, too, that the same experience always gives birth to the same sort of belief or religion. One revelation has been made to the Indian, another to the white man. I have much to learn of the Indian, nothing of the missionary. I am not sure but all that would tempt me to teach the Indian my religion would be his promise to teach me *his*. Long enough I had heard of irrelevant things; now at length I was glad to make acquaintance with the light that dwells in rotten wood.

I kept those little chips and wet them again the next night, but they emitted no light.

CHAPTER III

Saturday, July 25

AT BREAKFAST, THE Indian, evidently curious to know what would be expected of him the next day, asked me how I spent the Sunday when at home. I told him that I commonly sat in my chamber reading, etc., in the forenoon, and went to walk in the afternoon. At which he shook his head and said, "Er, that is ver' bad."

"How do you spend it?" I asked.

He said that he did no work, that he went to church at Oldtown when he was at home; in short, he did as he had been taught by the whites.

When we were washing the dishes in the lakes, many fishes came close up to us to get the particles of grease.

The weather seemed to be more settled this morning, and we set out early in order to finish our voyage up the lake before the wind arose. Soon after starting, the Indian directed our attention to the Northeast Carry, which we could plainly see, about thirteen miles distant. This carry is a rude wooden railroad running north and south about two miles, perfectly straight, from the lake to the Penobscot through a low tract, with a clearing three or four rods wide. This opening appeared as a clear bright, or light, point in the horizon, resting on the edge of the lake. We should not have suspected it to be visible if the Indian had not drawn our attention to it. It was a remarkable kind of light to steer for—daylight seen through a vista in the forest—but visible as far as an ordinary beacon by night.

We crossed a deep wide bay north of Kineo, leaving an island on our left and keeping up the eastern side of the lake. We then crossed another broad bay, which, as we could no longer observe the shore particularly, afforded ample time for conversation. The Indian said that he had got his money by hunting, mostly high up the West Branch of the Penobscot, and toward the head of the St. John. He had hunted there from a boy, and knew all about that region. His game had been beaver, otter, black cat (or fisher), sable, moose, etc. Canada lynx were plenty yet in burnt grounds. For food in the woods he uses partridges, ducks, dried moose meat, hedgehog, etc. Loons, too, were good, only "bile 'em good."

Pointing into the bay he said that it was the way to various lakes which he knew. Only solemn bear-haunted mountains with their great wooded slopes were visible. The Indian said that he had been along there several times. I asked him how he guided himself in the woods.

"Oh," said he, "I can tell good many ways."

When I pressed him further he answered, "Sometimes I lookum sidehill," and he glanced toward a high hill or mountain on the eastern shore; "great difference between the north and south; see where the sun has shone most. So trees—the large limbs bend toward south. Sometimes I lookum locks" (rocks).

I asked what he saw on the rocks, but he did not describe anything in particular, answering vaguely, in a mysterious or drawling tone, "bare locks on lake shore—great difference between north, south, east, west side—can tell what the sun has shone on."

"Suppose," said I, "that I should take you in a dark night right up here into the middle of the woods a hundred miles, set you down, and turn you round quickly twenty times, could you steer straight to Oldtown?"

"Oh, yer," said he, "have done pretty much same thing. I will tell you. Some years ago I met an old white hunter at Millinocket; very good hunter. He said he could go anywhere in the woods. He wanted to hunt with me that day, so we start. We chase a moose all the forenoon, round and round, till middle of afternoon, when we kill him. Then I said to him, 'Now you go straight to camp.'

"He said, 'I can't do that. I don't know where I am.'

"'Where you think camp?' I asked.

"He pointed so. Then I laugh at him. I take the lead and go right off the other way, cross our tracks many times, straight camp."

"How do you do that?" asked I.

"Oh, I can't tell *you*," he replied. "Great difference between me and white man."

It appeared as if the sources of information were so various that he did not give a distinct conscious attention to any one, and so could not readily refer to any when questioned about it, but he found his way very much as an animal does. Perhaps what is commonly called instinct in the animal in this case is merely a sharpened and educated sense. Often, when an Indian says, "I don't know," in regard to the route he is to take, he does not mean what a white man would by those words, for his Indian instinct may tell him still as much as the most confident white man knows. He does not carry things in his head, nor remember the route exactly, like a white man, but relies on himself at the moment. Not having experienced the need of the other sort of knowledge—all labeled and arranged—he has not acquired it.

The hunter with whom I talked in the stage knew some of the resources of the Indian. He said that he steered by the wind, or by the limbs of the hemlocks, which were largest on the south side; also sometimes, when he knew that there was a lake near, by firing his gun and listening to hear the direction and distance of the echo from over it.

As the forenoon advanced the wind increased. The last bay which we crossed before reaching the desolate pier at the Northeast Carry, was two or three miles over, and the wind was southwesterly. After going a third of the way, the waves had increased so as occasionally to wash into the canoe, and we saw that it was worse ahead. At first we might have turned about, but were not willing to. It would have been of no use to follow the course of the shore, for the waves ran still higher there on account of the greater sweep the wind had. At any rate it would have been dangerous now to alter our course, because the waves would have struck us at an advantage. It will not do to meet them at right angles, for then they will wash in both sides, but you must take them quartering. So the Indian stood up in the canoe and exerted all his skill and strength for a mile or two, while I paddled right along in order to give him more steerage-way. For more than a mile he did not allow a single wave to strike the canoe as it would, but turned it quickly from this side to that, so that it would always be on or near the crest of a wave when it broke, where all its force was spent, and we merely settled down with it. At length I jumped out onto the end of the pier against which the waves were dashing violently, in order to lighten the canoe and catch it at the landing, which was not much sheltered, but just as I jumped we took in two or three gallons of water. I remarked to the Indian, "You managed that well," to which he replied: "Ver' few men do that. Great many waves; when I look out for one, another come quick."

While the Indian went to get cedar bark, etc., to carry his canoe with, we cooked the dinner on the shore in the midst of a sprinkling rain. He prepared his canoe for carrying in this wise. He took a cedar shingle or splint eighteen inches long and four or five wide, rounded at one end, that the corners might not be in the way, and tied it with cedar bark by two holes made midway, near the edge on each side, to the middle crossbar of the canoe. When the canoe was lifted upon his head bottom up, this shingle, with its rounded end uppermost, distributed the weight over his shoulders and head, while a band of cedar bark, tied to the crossbar on each side of the shingle, passed round his breast, and another longer one, outside of the last, round his forehead; also a hand on each side rail served to steer the canoe and keep it from rocking. He thus carried it with his shoulders, head, breast, forehead, and both hands, as if the upper part of his body were all one hand to clasp and hold it. A cedar tree furnished all the gear in this case, as it had the woodwork of the canoe. One of the paddles rested on the crossbars in the bows. I took the canoe upon my head and found that I could carry it with ease, but I let him carry it, not caring to establish a different precedent. This shingle remained tied to the crossbar throughout the voyage, was always ready for the carries, and also served to protect the back of one passenger.

We were obliged to go over this carry twice, our load was so great. But the carries were an agreeable variety, and we improved the opportunity to gather the rare plants which we had seen, when we returned empty-handed.

We reached the Penobscot about four o'clock, and found there some St. Francis Indians encamped on the bank. They were making a canoe and drying moose meat. Their camp was covered with spruce bark. They had a young moose, taken in the river a fortnight before, confined in a sort of cage of logs piled up cob-fashion, seven or eight feet high. It was quite tame, about four feet high, and covered with moose flies. There was a large quantity of cornel, red maple, and also willow and aspen boughs, stuck through between the logs on all sides, butt ends out, and on their leaves it was browsing. It looked at first as if it were in a bower rather than a pen.

Our Indian said that *he* used *black* spruce roots to sew canoes with, obtaining it from high lands or mountains. The St. Francis Indians thought that *white* spruce roots might be best. But the former said, "No good, break, can't split 'em."

I told him I thought that I could make a canoe, but he expressed great doubt of it; at any rate he thought that my work would not be "neat" the first time.

Having reloaded, we paddled down the Penobscot. We saw a splendid yellow lily by the shore, which I plucked. It was six feet high and had twelve flowers, in two whorls, forming a pyramid. We afterward saw many more thus tall along this stream, and on the East Branch. The Indian said that the roots were good for soup, that is, to cook with meat, to thicken it, taking the place of flour. They get them in the fall. I dug some, and found a mass of bulbs pretty deep in the earth, two inches in diameter, looking, and even tasting, somewhat like raw green corn on the ear.

When we had gone about three miles down the Penobscot, we saw through the tree-tops a thunder-shower coming up in the west, and we looked out a camping-place in good season, about five o'clock.

I will describe the routine of camping. We generally told the Indian that we would stop at the first suitable place, so that he might be on the lookout for it. Having observed a clear, hard, and flat beach to land on, free from mud, and from stones which would injure the canoe, one would run up the bank to see if there were open and level space enough for the camp between the trees, or if it could be easily cleared, preferring at the same time a cool place, on account of insects. Sometimes we paddled a mile or more before finding one to our minds, for where the shore was suitable the bank would often be too steep, or else too low and grassy, and therefore mosquitoey. We then took out the baggage and drew up the canoe. The Indian cut a path to the spot we had selected, which was usually within two or three rods of the water, and we carried up our baggage.

One, perhaps, takes birch bark, always at hand, and dead dry wood, and kindles a fire five or six feet in front of where we intend to lie. It matters not, commonly, on which side this is, because there is little or no wind in so dense a wood at that season; and then he gets a kettle of water from the river, and takes out the pork, bread, coffee, etc., from their several packages.

Another, meanwhile, having the axe, cuts down the nearest dead rock maple or other dry hard wood, collecting several large logs to last through the night, also a green stake, with a notch or fork to it, which is slanted over the fire, perhaps resting on a rock or forked stake, to hang the kettle on, and two forked stakes and a pole for the tent.

The third man pitches the tent, cuts a dozen or more pins with his knife to fasten it down with, and then collects an armful or two of fir twigs, arbor-vitæ, spruce, or hemlock, whichever is at hand, and makes the bed, beginning at either end, and laying the twigs wrong side up, in regular rows, covering the stub ends of the last row; first, however, filling the hollows, if there are any, with coarser material.

Commonly, by the time the bed is made, or within fifteen or twenty minutes, the water boils, the pork is fried, and supper is ready. We eat this sitting on the ground, or a stump, around a large piece of birch bark for a table, each holding a dipper in one hand and a piece of ship-bread or fried pork in the other, frequently making a pass with his hand, or thrusting his head into the smoke, to avoid the mosquitoes.

Next, pipes are lit by those who smoke, and veils are donned by those who have them, and we hastily examine and dry our plants, anoint our faces and hands, and go to bed.

Though you have nothing to do but see the country, there's rarely any time to spare, hardly enough to examine a plant, before the night or drowsiness is upon you.

Such was the ordinary experience, but this evening we had camped earlier on account of the rain, and had more time. We found that our camp was on an old indistinct supply-road, running along the river. What is called a road there shows no ruts or trace of wheels, for they are not used; nor, indeed, of runners, since they are used only in the winter when the snow is several feet deep. It is only an indistinct vista through the wood, which it takes an experienced eye to detect.

We had no sooner pitched our tent than the thunder-shower burst on us, and we hastily crept under it, drawing our bags after us, curious to see how much of a shelter our thin cotton roof was going to be in this excursion. Though the violence of the rain forced a fine shower through the cloth before it was fairly wetted and shrunk, with which we were well bedewed, we managed to keep pretty dry, only a box of matches having been left out and spoiled, and before we were aware of it the shower was over, and only the dripping trees imprisoned us.

Wishing to see what fishes were in the river there, we cast our lines over the wet bushes on the shore, but they were repeatedly swept down the swift stream in vain. So, leaving the Indian, we took the canoe, just before dark, and dropped down the river a few rods to fish at the mouth of a sluggish brook. We pushed up this a rod or two, but were soon driven off by the mosquitoes. While there we heard the Indian fire his gun twice in rapid succession. His object was to clean out and dry it after the rain, and he then loaded it with ball, being now on ground where he expected to meet with large game. This sudden loud crashing noise in the still aisles of the forest affected me like an insult to nature, or ill manners at any rate, as if you were to fire a gun in a hall or temple. It was not heard far, however, except along the river, the sound being rapidly hushed up or absorbed by the damp trees and mossy ground.

The Indian made a little smothered fire of damp leaves close to the back of the camp, that the smoke might drive through and keep out the mosquitoes, but just before we fell asleep this suddenly blazed up and came near setting fire to the tent.

CHAPTER IV

Sunday, July 26

THE NOTE OF the white-throated sparrow was the first heard in the morning, and with this all the woods rang. Though commonly unseen, their simple *ah, te-te-te, te-te-te, te-te-te*, so sharp and piercing, was as distinct to the ear as the passage of a spark of fire shot into the darkest of the forest would be to the eye. We were commonly aroused by their lively strain very early. What a glorious time they must have in that wilderness, far from mankind!

I told the Indian that we would go to church to Chesuncook this morning, some fifteen miles. It was settled weather at last. A few swallows flitted over the water, we heard Maryland yellow-throats along the shore, the notes of the chickadee, and, I believe, redstarts. Moose-flies of large size pursued us in midstream.

The Indian thought that we should lie by on Sunday. Said he, "We come here lookum things, look all round, but come Sunday look up all that, and then Monday look again."

He spoke of an Indian of his acquaintance who had been with some ministers to Katahdin and had told him how they conducted. This he described in a low and solemn voice. "They make a long prayer every morning and night, and at every meal. Come Sunday, they stop 'em, no go at all that day—keep still—preach all day—first one, then another, just like church. Oh, ver' good men.

One day going along a river, they came to the body of
a man in the water, drowned good while. They go right
ashore—stop there, go no farther that day—they have
meeting there, preach and pray just like Sunday. Then they
go back and carry the body with them. Oh, they ver'
good men."

I judged from this account that their every camp was
a camp-meeting, and that they wanted an opportunity to
preach somewhere more than to see Katahdin.

However, the Indian added, plying the paddle all the
while, that if we would go along he must go with us, he
our man, and he suppose that if he no takum pay for
what he do Sunday then ther's no harm, but if he takum
pay then wrong. I told him that he was stricter than white
men. Nevertheless, I noticed that he did not forget to
reckon in the Sundays at last.

He appeared to be a very religious man, and said his
prayers in a loud voice, in Indian, kneeling before the
camp, morning and evening—sometimes scrambling up
in haste when he had forgotten this, and saying them with
great rapidity. In the course of the day he remarked, "Poor
man rememberum God more than rich."

We soon passed the island where I had camped four
years before. The deadwater, a mile or two below it, the
Indian said was "a great place for moose." We saw the
grass bent where a moose came out the night before, and
the Indian said that he could smell one as far as he could
see him, but he added that if he should see five or six
to-day close by canoe he no shoot 'em. Accordingly, as
he was the only one of the party who had a gun, or had
come a-hunting, the moose were safe.

Just below this a cat owl flew heavily over the stream, and he, asking if I knew what it was, imitated very well the common *hoo, hoo, hoo, hoorer, hoo*, of our woods.

We carried a part of the baggage about Pine Stream Falls, while the Indian went down in the canoe. A Bangor merchant had told us that two men in his employ were drowned some time ago while passing these falls in a bateau, and a third clung to a rock all night and was taken off in the morning. There were magnificent great purple fringed orchises on this carry and the neighboring shores. I measured the largest canoe birch which I saw in this journey near the end of the carry. It was fourteen and one half feet in circumference at two feet from the ground, but at five feet divided into three parts. The Indian cut a small woody knob as big as a filbert from the trunk of a fir, apparently an old balsam vesicle filled with wood, which he said was good medicine.

After we had embarked and gone half a mile, my companion remembered that he had left his knife, and we paddled back to get it, against the strong and swift current. This taught us the difference between going up and down the stream, for while we were working our way back a quarter of a mile, we should have gone down a mile and half at least. So we landed, and while he and the Indian were gone back for it, I watched the motions of the foam, a kind of white waterfowl near the shore, forty or fifty rods below. It alternately appeared and disappeared behind the rock, being carried round by an eddy.

Immediately below these falls was the Chesuncook Deadwater, caused by the flowing back of the lake. As we paddled slowly over this, the Indian told us a story of his hunting thereabouts, and something more interesting about himself. It appeared that he had represented his tribe at Augusta, and once at Washington. He had a great idea of education, and would occasionally break out into such expressions as this, "Kademy—good thing—I suppose they usum Fifth Reader there. You been college?"

We steered across the northwest end of the lake. It is an agreeable change to cross a lake after you have been shut up in the woods, not only on account of the greater expanse of water, but also of sky. It is one of the surprises which Nature has in store for the traveler in the forest. To look down, in this case, over eighteen miles of water was liberating and civilizing even. The lakes also reveal the mountains, and give ample scope and range to our thought. Already there were half a dozen log huts about this end of the lake, though so far from a road. In these woods the earliest settlements are clustering about the lakes, partly, I think, for the sake of the neighborhood as the oldest clearings. Water is a pioneer which the settler follows, taking advantage of its improvements.

About noon we turned northward up a broad kind of estuary, and at its northeast corner found the Caucomgomoc River, and after going about a mile from the lake reached the Umbazookskus. Our course was up the Umbazookskus, but as the Indian knew of a good camping-place, that is, a cool place where there were few mosquitoes, about half a mile farther up the Caucomgomoc, we went thither. So quickly we changed the civilizing sky of Chesuncook for the dark wood of the Caucomgomoc. On reaching the Indian's camping-ground on the south side, where the bank was about a dozen feet high, I read on the trunk of a fir tree blazed by an axe an inscription in charcoal which had been left by him. It was surmounted by a drawing of a bear paddling a canoe, which he said was the sign used by his family always. The drawing, though rude, could not be mistaken for anything but a bear, and he doubted my ability to copy it. The inscription ran thus. I interline the English of his Indian as he gave it to me.

(The figure of a bear in a boat.)
July 26
1853

~

niasoseb
We alone Joseph
Polis elioi
Polis start
sia olta
for Oldtown
onke ni
right away
quambi

July 15
1855
Niasoseb

He added now below: —

1857
July 26
Jo. Polis

This was one of his homes. I saw where he had sometimes stretched his moose-hides on the sunny north side of the river where there was a narrow meadow.

After we had selected a place for our camp, and kindled our fire, almost exactly on the site of the Indian's last camp here, he, looking up, observed, "That tree danger."

It was a dead part, more than a foot in diameter, of a large canoe birch, which branched at the ground. This branch, rising thirty feet or more, slanted directly over the spot which we had chosen for our bed. I told him to try it with his axe, but he could not shake it perceptibly, and, therefore, seemed inclined to disregard it, and my companion expressed his willingness to run the risk. But it seemed to me that we should be fools to lie under it, for though the lower part was firm, the top, for aught we knew, might be just ready to fall, and we should at any rate be very uneasy if the wind arose in the night. It is a common accident for men camping in the woods to be killed by a falling tree. So the camp was moved to the other side of the fire.

The Indian said that the Umbazookskus, being a dead stream with broad meadows, was a good place for moose, and he frequently came a-hunting here, being out alone three weeks or more from Oldtown. He sometimes, also, went a-hunting to the Seboois Lakes, taking the stage, with his gun and ammunition, axe and blankets, hard-bread and pork, perhaps for a hundred miles of the way, and jumped off at the wildest place on the road, where he was at once at home, and every rod was a tavern-site for him. Then, after a short journey through the woods, he would build a spruce-bark canoe in one day, putting but few ribs into it, that it might be light, and, after doing his hunting with it on the lakes, would return with his furs the same way he had come. Thus you have an Indian availing himself of the advantages of civilization, without losing any of his woodcraft, but proving himself the more successful hunter for it.

This man was very clever and quick to learn anything in his line. Our tent was of a kind new to him, but when he had once seen it pitched it was surprising how quickly he would find and prepare the pole and forked stakes to pitch it with, cutting and placing them right the first time, though I am sure that the majority of white men would have blundered several times.

Now I thought I would observe how he spent his Sunday. While I and my companion were looking about at the trees and river he went to sleep. Indeed, he improved every opportunity to get a nap, whatever the day.

Rambling about the woods at this camp, I noticed that they consisted chiefly of firs, spruce, red maple, birch, and, along the river, the hoary alder. I could trace the outlines of large birches that had fallen long ago, collapsed and rotted and turned to soil, by faint yellowish-green lines of featherlike moss, eighteen inches wide and twenty or thirty feet long, crossed by other similar lines.

Wild as it was, it was hard for me to get rid of the associations of the settlements. Any steady and monotonous sound, to which I did not distinctly attend, passed for a sound of human industry. The waterfalls which I heard were not without their dams and mills to my imagination; and several times I found that I had been regarding the steady rushing sound of the wind from over the woods beyond the rivers as that of a train of cars. Our minds anywhere, when left to themselves, are always thus busily drawing conclusions from false premises.

I asked the Indian to make us a sugar-bowl of birch bark, which he did, using the great knife which dangled in a sheath from his belt; but the bark broke at the corners when he bent it up, and he said it was not good—that there was a great difference in this respect between the bark of one canoe birch and that of another.

My companion, wishing to distinguish between the black and white spruce, asked Polis to show him a twig of the latter, which he did at once, together with the black; indeed, he could distinguish them about as far as he could see them. As the two twigs appeared very much alike, my companion asked the Indian to point out the difference; whereupon the latter, taking the twigs, instantly remarked, as he passed his hand over them successively in a stroking manner, that the white was rough, that is, the needles stood up nearly perpendicular, but the black smooth, that is, as if bent down. This was an obvious difference, both to sight and touch.

I asked him to get some black spruce root and make some thread. Whereupon, without looking up at the trees overhead, he began to grub in the ground, instantly distinguishing the black spruce roots, and cutting off a slender one, three or four feet long, and as big as a pipestem, he split the end with his knife, and taking a half between the thumb and forefinger of each hand, rapidly separated its whole length into two equal semi-cylindrical halves. Then, giving me another root, he said, "You try."

But in my hands it immediately ran off one side, and I got only a very short piece. Though it looked easy, I found that there was a great art in splitting these roots. The split is skillfully humored by bending short with this hand or that, and so kept in the middle. He then took off the bark from each half, pressing a short piece of cedar bark against the convex side with both hands, while he drew the root upward with his teeth. An Indian's teeth are strong, and I noticed that he used his often where we should have used a hand. They amounted to a third hand. He thus obtained in a moment a very neat, tough, and flexible string, which he could tie into a knot, or make into a fishline even. He said that you would be obliged to give half a dollar for spruce root enough for a canoe, thus prepared.

He had discovered the day before that his canoe leaked a little, and said that it was owing to stepping into it violently. I asked him where he would get pitch to mend it with, for they commonly use hard pitch, obtained of the whites at Oldtown. He said that he could make something very similar, and equally good, of material which we had with us; and he wished me to guess what. But I could not, and he would not tell me, though he showed me a ball of it when made, as big as a pea and like black pitch, saying, at last, that there were some things which a man did not tell even his wife.

Being curious to see what kind of fishes there were in this dark, deep, sluggish river, I cast in my line just before night, and caught several small sucker-like fishes, which the Indian at once rejected, saying that they were good for nothing. Also, he would not touch a pout, which I caught, and said that neither Indians nor whites thereabouts ever ate them. But he said that some small silvery fishes, which I called white chivin, were the best fish in the Penobscot waters, and if I would toss them up the bank to him, he would cook them for me. After cleaning them, not very carefully, leaving the heads on, he laid them on the coals and so broiled them.

Returning from a short walk, he brought a vine in his hand, saying that it made the best tea of anything in the woods. It was the creeping snowberry, which was quite common there, its berries just grown. So we determined to have some tea made of this. It had a slight checkerberry flavor, and we both agreed that it was really better than the black tea which we had brought. We thought it quite a discovery, and that it might well be dried and sold in the shops. I for one, however, am not an old tea-drinker and cannot speak with authority to others. The Indian said that they also used for tea a certain herb which grew in low ground, which he did not find there, and Labrador tea; also hemlock leaves, the last especially in winter when the other plants were covered with snow; and various other things. We could have had a new kind of tea every night.

Just before night we saw a *musquash*, the only one we saw in this voyage, swimming downward on the opposite side of the stream. The Indian, wishing to get one to eat, hushed us, saying, "Stop, me call 'em"; and, sitting flat on the bank, he began to make a curious squeaking, wiry sound with his lips, exerting himself considerably. I was greatly surprised—thought that I had at last got into the wilderness, and that he was a wild man indeed, to be talking to a musquash! I did not know which of the two was the strangest to me. He seemed suddenly to have quite forsaken humanity, and gone over to the musquash side. The musquash, however, as near as I could see, did not turn aside, and the Indian said that he saw our fire; but it was evident that he was in the habit of calling the musquash to him, as he said. An acquaintance of mine who was hunting moose in these woods a month after this, tells me that his Indian in this way repeatedly called the musquash within reach of his paddle in the moonlight, and struck at them.

The Indian said a particularly long prayer this Sunday evening, as if to atone for working in the morning.

CHAPTER V

Monday, July 27

HAVING RAPIDLY LOADED the canoe, which the Indian always carefully attended to, that it might be well trimmed, and each having taken a look, as usual, to see that nothing was left, we set out again, descending the Caucomgomoc, and turning northeasterly up the Umbazookskus. This name, the Indian said, meant *Much Meadow River.* We found it now very wide on account of the rains. The space between the woods, chiefly bare meadow, was from fifty to two hundred rods in breadth.

In the water on the meadows grew sedges, wool-grass, the common blue flag abundantly, its flower just showing itself above the high water, as if it were a blue water-lily, and higher in the meadows a great many clumps of a peculiar narrow-leaved willow. Here also grew the red osier, its large fruit now whitish.

It was unusual for the woods to be so distant from the shore, and there was quite an echo from them, but when I was shouting in order to awake it, the Indian reminded me that I should scare the moose, which he was looking out for, and which we all wanted to see.

Having paddled several miles up the Umbazookskus, it suddenly contracted to a mere brook, narrow and swift, the larches and other trees approaching the bank and leaving no open meadow. We landed to get a black spruce pole for pushing against the stream. The one selected was quite slender, cut about ten feet long, merely whittled to a point, and the bark shaved off.

While we were thus employed, two Indians in a canoe hove in sight round the bushes, coming down stream. Our Indian knew one of them, an old man, and fell into conversation with him. He belonged at the foot of Moosehead. The other was of another tribe. They were returning from hunting. I asked the younger if they had seen any moose, to which he said "No"; but I, seeing the moose-hides sticking out from a great bundle made with their blankets in the middle of the canoe, added, "Only their hides."

As he was a foreigner, he may have wished to deceive me, for it is against the law for white men and foreigners to kill moose in Maine at this season. But perhaps he need not have been alarmed, for the moose-wardens are not very particular. I heard of one who, being asked by a white man going into the woods what he would say if he killed a moose, answered, "If you bring me a quarter of it I guess you won't be troubled." His duty being, as he said, only to prevent the "indiscriminate" slaughter of them for their hides. I suppose that he would consider it an *indiscriminate* slaughter when a quarter was not reserved for himself.

We continued along through the most extensive larch wood which I had seen—tall and slender trees with fantastic branches. You do not find straggling trees of this species here and there throughout the wood, but rather a little forest of them. The same is the case with the white and red pines and some other trees, greatly to the convenience of the lumberer. They are of a social habit, growing in "veins," "clumps," "groups," or "communities," as the explorers call them, distinguishing them far away, from the top of a hill or a tree, the white pines towering above the surrounding forest, or else they form extensive forests by themselves. I should have liked to come across a large community of pines which had never been invaded by the lumbering army.

We saw some fresh moose-tracks along the shore. The stream was only from one and one half to three rods wide, quite winding, with occasional small islands, meadows, and some very swift and shallow places. When we came to an island the Indian never hesitated which side to take, as if the current told him which was the shortest and deepest. It was lucky for us that the water was so high. We had to walk but once on this stream, carrying a part of the load, at a swift and shallow reach, while he got up with the canoe, not being obliged to take out, though he said it was very strong water. Once or twice we passed the red wreck of a bateau which had been stove some spring.

While making this portage I saw many splendid specimens of the great purple fringed orchis, three feet high. It is remarkable that such delicate flowers should here adorn these wilderness paths.

The Umbazookskus is called ten miles long. Having poled up the narrowest part some three or four miles, the next opening in the sky was over Umbazookskus Lake, which we suddenly entered about eleven o'clock in the forenoon. It stretches north-westerly four or five miles. We crossedthe southeast end to the carry into Mud Pond.

Hodge, who went through this way to the St. Lawrence in the service of the State, calls the portage here a mile and three quarters long. The Indian said this was the wettest carry in the State, and as the season was a very wet one we anticipated an unpleasant walk. As usual he made one large bundle of the pork-keg, cooking-utensils, and other loose traps, by tying them up in his blanket. We should be obliged to go over the carry twice, and our method was to carry one half part way, and then go back for the rest.

Our path ran close by the door of a log hut in a clearing at this end of the carry, which the Indian, who alone entered it, found to be occupied by a Canadian and his family, and that the man had been blind for a year. This was the first house above Chesuncook, and was built here, no doubt, because it was the route of the lumberers in the winter and spring.

After a slight ascent from the lake through the springy soil of the Canadian's clearing, we entered on a level and very wet and rocky path through the dense evergreen forest, a loosely paved gutter merely, where we went leaping from rock to rock and from side to side in the vain attempt to keep out of the water and mud. It was on this carry that the white hunter whom I met in the stage, as he told me, had shot two bears a few months before. They stood directly in the path and did not turn out for him. He said that at this season bears were found on the mountains and hillsides in search of berries and were apt to be saucy.

Here commences what was called, twenty years ago, the best timber land in the State. This very spot was described as "covered with the greatest abundance of pine," but now this appeared to me, comparatively, an uncommon tree there—and yet you did not see where any more could have stood, amid the dense growth of cedar, fir, etc.

The Indian with his canoe soon disappeared before us, but ere long he came back and told us to take a path which turned off westward, it being better walking, and, at my suggestion, he agreed to leave a bough in the regular carry at that place that we might not pass it by mistake. Thereafter, he said, we were to keep the main path, and he added, "You see 'em my tracks."

But I had not much faith that we could distinguish his tracks, since others had passed over the carry within a few days. We turned off at the right place, but were soon confused by numerous logging-paths coming into the one we were on. However, we kept what we considered the main path, though it was a winding one, and in this, at long intervals, we distinguished a faint trace of a footstep. This, though comparatively unworn, was at first a better, or, at least, a dryer road than the regular carry which we had left. It led through an arbor-vitæ wilderness of the grimmest character. The great fallen and rotting trees had been cut through and rolled aside, and their huge trunks abutted on the path on each side, while others still lay across it two or three feet high.

It was impossible for us to discern the Indian's trail in the elastic moss, which, like a thick carpet, covered every rock and fallen tree, as well as the earth. Nevertheless, I did occasionally detect the track of a man, and I gave myself some credit for it. I carried my whole load at once, a heavy knapsack, and a large rubber bag containing our bread and a blanket, swung on a paddle, in all about sixty pounds; but my companion preferred to make two journeys by short stages while I waited for him. We could not be sure that we were not depositing our loads each time farther off from the true path.

As I sat waiting for my companion, he would seem to be gone a long time, and I had ample opportunity to make observations on the forest. I now first began to be seriously molested by the black fly, a very small but perfectly formed fly of that color, about one tenth of an inch long, which I felt, and then saw, in swarms about me, as I sat by a wider and more than usually doubtful fork in this dark forest path. Remembering that I had a wash in my knapsack, prepared by a thoughtful hand in Bangor, I made haste to apply it to my face and hands, and was glad to find it effectual, as long as it was fresh, or for twenty minutes, not only against black flies, but all the insects that molested us. They would not alight on the part thus defended. It was composed of sweet oil and oil of turpentine, with a little oil of spearmint, and camphor. However, I finally concluded that the remedy was worse than the disease, it was so disagreeable and inconvenient to have your face and hands covered with such a mixture.

Three large slate-colored birds of the jay genus, the Canada jay, came flitting silently and by degrees toward me, and hopped down the limbs inquisitively to within seven or eight feet. Fish hawks from the lake uttered their sharp whistling notes low over the top of the forest near me, as if they were anxious about a nest there.

After I had sat there some time I noticed at this fork in the path a tree which had been blazed, and the letters "Chamb. L." written on it with red chalk. This I knew to mean Chamberlain Lake. So I concluded that on the whole we were on the right course.

My companion having returned with his bag, we set forward again. The walking rapidly grew worse and the path more indistinct, and at length we found ourselves in a more open and regular swamp made less passable than ordinary by the unusual wetness of the season. We sank a foot deep in water and mud at every step, and sometimes up to our knees. The trail was almost obliterated, being no more than a musquash leaves in similar places when he parts the floating sedge. In fact, it probably was a musquash trail in some places. We concluded that if Mud Pond was as muddy as the approach to it was wet, it certainly deserved its name. It would have been amusing to behold the dogged and deliberate pace at which we entered that swamp, without interchanging a word, as if determined to go through it, though it should come up to our necks. Having penetrated a considerable distance into this and found a tussock on which we could deposit our loads, though there was no place to sit, my companion went back for the rest of his pack.

After a long while my companion came back, and the Indian with him. We had taken the wrong road, and the Indian had lost us. He had gone back to the Canadian's camp and asked him which way we had probably gone, since he could better understand the ways of white men, and he told him correctly that we had undoubtedly taken the supply road to Chamberlain Lake. The Indian was greatly surprised that we should have taken what he called a "tow," that is, tote, toting, or supply, road instead of a carry path,—that we had not followed his tracks,—said it was "strange," and evidently thought little of our woodcraft.

Having held a consultation and eaten a mouthful of bread, we concluded that it would perhaps be nearer for us two now to keep on to Chamberlain Lake, omitting Mud Pond, than to go back and start anew for the last place, though the Indian had never been through this way and knew nothing about it. In the meanwhile he would go back and finish carrying over his canoe and bundle to Mud Pond, cross that, and go down its outlet and up Chamberlain Lake, and trust to meet us there before night. It was now a little after noon. He supposed that the water in which we stood had flowed back from Mud Pond, which could not be far off eastward, but was unapproachable through the dense cedar swamp.

Keeping on, we were ere long agreeably disappointed by reaching firmer ground, and we crossed a ridge where the path was more distinct, but there was never any outlook over the forest. At one place I heard a very clear and piercing note from a small hawk as he dashed through the tree-tops over my head. We also saw and heard several times the red squirrel. This, according to the Indian, is the only squirrel found in those woods, except a very few striped ones. It must have a solitary time in that dark evergreen forest, where there is so little life, seventy-five miles from a road as we had come. I wondered how he could call any particular tree there his home, and yet he would run up the stem of one out of the myriads, as if it were an old road to him. I fancied that he must be glad to see us, though he did seem to chide us. One of those somber fir and spruce woods is not complete unless you hear from out its cavernous mossy and twiggy recesses his fine alarum—his spruce voice, like the working of the sap through some crack in a tree. Such an impertinent fellow would occasionally try to alarm the wood about me.

"Oh," said I, "I am well acquainted with your family. I know your cousins in Concord very well." But my overtures were vain, for he would withdraw by his aerial turnpikes into a more distant cedar-top, and spring his rattle again.

We entered another swamp, at a necessarily slow pace, where the walking was worse than ever, not only on account of the water, but the fallen timber, which often obliterated the indistinct trail entirely. The fallen trees were so numerous that for long distances the route was through a succession of small yards, where we climbed over fences as high as our heads, down into water often up to our knees, and then over another fence into a second yard, and so on. In many places the canoe would have run if it had not been for the fallen timber. Again it would be more open, but equally wet, too wet for trees to grow. It was a mossy swamp, which it required the long legs of a moose to traverse, and it is very likely that we scared some of them in our transit, though we saw none. It was ready to echo the growl of a bear, the howl of a wolf, or the scream of a panther; but when you get fairly into the middle of one of these grim forests you are surprised to find that the larger inhabitants are not at home commonly, but have left only a puny red squirrel to bark at you. Generally speaking, a howling wilderness does not howl; it is the imagination of the traveler that does the howling. I did, however, see one dead porcupine. Perhaps he had succumbed to the difficulties of the way. These bristly fellows are a very suitable small fruit of such unkempt wildernesses.

Making a logging-road in the Maine woods is called "swamping" it, and they who do the work are called "swampers." I now perceived the fitness of the term. This was the most perfectly swamped of all the roads I ever saw. Nature must have coöperated with art here. However, I suppose they would tell you that this name took its origin from the fact that the chief work of roadmakers in those woods is to make the swamps passable. We came to a stream where the bridge, which had been made of logs tied together with cedar bark, had been broken up, and we got over as we could. Such as it was, this ruined bridge was the chief evidence that we were on a path of any kind.

We then crossed another low rising ground, and I, who wore shoes, had an opportunity to wring out my stockings, but my companion, who used boots, had found that this was not a safe experiment for him, for he might not be able to get his wet boots on again. He went over the whole ground, or water, three times, for which reason our progress was very slow. Beside that, the water softened our feet, and to some extent unfitted them for walking.

As I sat waiting for him it would naturally seem an unaccountable time that he was gone. Therefore, as I could see through the woods that the sun was getting low, and it was uncertain how far the lake might be, even if we were on the right course, and in what part of the world we should find ourselves at nightfall, I proposed that I should push through with what speed I could, leaving boughs to mark my path, and find the lake and the Indian, if possible, before night, and send the latter back to carry my companion's bag.

Having gone about a mile I heard a noise like the note of an owl, which I soon discovered to be made by the Indian, and answering him, we soon came together. He had reached the lake after crossing Mud Pond and running some rapids below it, and had come up about a mile and a half on our path. If he had not come back to meet us, we probably should not have found him that night, for the path branched once or twice before reaching this particular part of the lake. So he went back for my companion and his bag. Having waded through another stream, where the bridge of logs had been broken up and half floated away, we continued on through alternate mud and water to the shores of Apmoojenegamook Lake, which we reached in season for a late supper, instead of dining there, as we had expected, having gone without our dinner.

It was at least five miles by the way we had come, and as my companion had gone over most of it three times he had walked full a dozen miles. In the winter, when the water is frozen and the snow is four feet deep, it is no doubt a tolerable path to a footman. If you want an exact recipe for making such a road, take one part Mud Pond, and dilute it with equal parts of Umbazookskus and Apmoojenegamook; then send a family of musquash through to locate it, look after the grades and culverts, and finish it to their minds, and let a hurricane follow to do the fencing.

We had come out on a point extending into Apmoojenegamook, or Chamberlain Lake, where there was a broad, gravelly, and rocky shore, encumbered with bleached logs and trees. We were rejoiced to see such dry things in that part of the world. But at first we did not attend to dryness so much as to mud and wetness. We all three walked into the lake up to our middle to wash our clothes.

This was another noble lake, twelve miles long; if you add Telos Lake, which, since the dam was built, has been connected with it by dead water, it will be twenty; and it is apparently from a mile and a half to two miles wide. We were about midway its length on the south side. We could see the only clearing in these parts, called the "Chamberlain Farm," with two or three log buildings close together, on the opposite shore, some two and a half miles distant. The smoke of our fire on the shore brought over two men in a canoe from the farm, that being a common signal agreed on when one wishes to cross. It took them about half an hour to come over, and they had their labor for their pains this time.

After putting on such dry clothes as we had, and hanging the others to dry on the pole which the Indian arranged over the fire, we ate our supper, and lay down on the pebbly shore with our feet to the fire without pitching our tent, making a thin bed of grass to cover the stones.

Here first I was molested by the little midge called the no-see-em, especially over the sand at the water's edge, for it is a kind of sand-fly. You would not observe them but for their light-colored wings. They are said to get under your clothes and produce a feverish heat, which I suppose was what I felt that night.

Our insect foes in this excursion were, first, mosquitoes, only troublesome at night, or when we sat still on shore by day; second, black flies (*simulium molestum*), which molested us more or less on the carries by day, and sometimes in narrower parts of the stream; third, moose-flies, stout brown flies much like a horsefly. They can bite smartly, according to Polis, but are easily avoided or killed. Fourth, the no-see-ems. Of all these, the mosquitoes are the only ones that troubled me seriously, but as I was provided with a wash and a veil, they have not made any deep impression.

The Indian would not use our wash to protect his face and hands, for fear that it would hurt his skin, nor had he any veil. He, therefore, suffered from insects throughout this journey more than either of us. He regularly tied up his face in his handkerchief, and buried it in his blanket, and he now finally lay down on the sand between us and the fire for the sake of the smoke, which he tried to make enter his blanket about his face, and for the same purpose he lit his pipe and breathed the smoke into his blanket.

In the middle of the night we heard the voice of the loon, loud and distinct, from far over the lake. It is a very wild sound, quite in keeping with the place and the circumstances of the traveler, and very unlike the voice of a bird. I could lie awake for hours listening to it, it is so thrilling. When camping in such a wilderness as this, you are prepared to hear sounds from some of its inhabitants which will give voice to its wildness. Some idea of bears, wolves, or panthers runs in your head naturally, and when this note is first heard very far off at midnight, as you lie with your ear to the ground,—the forest being perfectly still about you, you take it for granted that it is the voice of a wolf or some other wild beast,—you conclude that it is a pack of wolves baying the moon, or, perchance, cantering after a moose. It was the unfailing and characteristic sound of those lakes.

Some friends of mine, who two years ago went up the Caucomgomoc River, were serenaded by wolves while moose-hunting by moonlight. It was a sudden burst, as if a hundred demons had broke loose,—a startling sound enough, which, if any, would make your hair stand on end,—and all was still again. It lasted but a moment, and you'd have thought there were twenty of them, when probably there were only two or three. They heard it twice only, and they said that it gave expression to the wilderness which it lacked before. I heard of some men, who, while skinning a moose lately in those woods, were driven off from the carcass by a pack of wolves, which ate it up.

This of the loon—I do not mean its laugh, but its looning—is a long-drawn call, as it were, sometimes singularly human to my ear—*hoo-hoo-ooooo*, like the hallooing of a man on a very high key, having thrown his voice into his head. I have heard a sound exactly like it when breathing heavily through my own nostrils, half awake at ten at night, suggesting my affinity to the loon; as if its language were but a dialect of my own, after all. Formerly, when lying awake at midnight in those woods, I had listened to hear some words or syllables of their language, but it chanced that I listened in vain until I heard the cry of the loon. I have heard it occasionally on the ponds of my native town, but there its wildness is not enhanced by the surrounding scenery.

I was awakened at midnight by some heavy, low-flying bird, probably a loon, flapping by close over my head along the shore. So, turning the other side of my half-clad body to the fire, I sought slumber again.

CHAPTER VI

Tuesday, July 28

WHEN WE AWOKE we found a heavy dew on our blankets. I lay awake very early and listened to the clear, shrill *ah, te te, te te, te* of the white-throated sparrow, repeated at short intervals, without the least variation, for half an hour, as if it could not enough express its happiness.

We did some more washing in the lake this morning, and, with our clothes hung about on the dead trees and rocks, the shore looked like washing-day at home. The Indian, taking the hint, borrowed the soap, and, walking into the lake, washed his only cotton shirt on his person, then put on his pants and let it dry on him.

I observed that he wore a cotton shirt, originally white, a greenish flannel one over it, but no waistcoat, flannel drawers, and strong linen or duck pants, which also had been white, blue woolen stockings, cowhide boots, and a Kossuth hat.★ He carried no change of clothing, but, putting on a stout, thick jacket, which he laid aside in the canoe, and seizing a full-sized axe, his gun and ammunition, and a blanket, which would do for a sail or knapsack, if wanted, and strapping on his belt, which contained a large sheath-knife, he walked off at once, ready to be gone

---

★ A soft felt hat of the kind worn by the Hungarian patriot, Kossuth, on his visit to this country in 1851-52.

all summer. This looked very independent—a few simple
and effective tools, and no rubber clothing. He was always
the first ready to start in the morning. Instead of carrying
a large bundle of his own extra clothing, etc., he brought
back the greatcoats of moose tied up in his blanket. I
found that his outfit was the result of a long experience,
and in the main hardly to be improved on, unless by
washing and an extra shirt. Wanting a button here, he
walked off to a place where some Indians had recently
encamped, and searched for one, but I believe in vain.

Having softened our stiffened boots and shoes with the
pork fat, the usual disposition of what was left at breakfast,
we crossed the lake, steering in a diagonal direction north-
eastly about four miles to the outlet. The Indian name,
Apmoojenegamook, means lake that is crossed, because
the usual course lies across and not along it. We did not
intend to go far down the Allegash, but merely to get a
view of the lakes which are its source, and then return
this way to the East Branch of the Penobscot.

After reaching the middle of the lake, we found the
waves pretty high, and the Indian warned my companion,
who was nodding, that he must not allow himself to fall
asleep in the canoe lest he should upset us; adding, that
when Indians want to sleep in a canoe, they lie down
straight on the bottom. But in this crowded one that was
impossible. However, he said that he would nudge him if
he saw him nodding.

A belt of dead trees stood all around the lake, some far
out in the water, with others prostrate behind them, and
they made the shore, for the most part, almost inaccessible.
This is the effect of the dam at the outlet. Thus the natural

sandy or rocky shore, with its green fringe, was concealed and destroyed. We coasted westward along the north side, searching for the outlet, about quarter of a mile distant from this savage-looking shore, on which the waves were breaking violently, knowing that it might easily be concealed amid this rubbish, or by the overlapping of the shore. It is remarkable how little these important gates to a lake are blazoned. There is no triumphal arch over the modest inlet or outlet, but at some undistinguished point it trickles in or out through the uninterrupted forest, almost as through a sponge.

We reached the outlet in about an hour, and carried over the dam there, which is quite a solid structure, and about one quarter of a mile farther there was a second dam. The result of this particular damming about Chamberlain Lake is that the headwaters of the St. John are made to flow by Bangor. They have thus dammed all the larger lakes, raising their broad surfaces many feet, thus turning the forces of Nature against herself, that they might float their spoils out of the country. They rapidly run out of these immense forests all the finer and more accessible pine timber, and then leave the bears to watch the decaying dams, not clearing nor cultivating the land, nor making roads, nor building houses, but leaving it a wilderness, as they found it. In many parts only these dams remain, like deserted beaver dams. Think how much land they have flowed without asking Nature's leave.

The wilderness experiences a sudden rise of all her streams and lakes. She feels ten thousand vermin gnawing at the base of her noblest trees. Many combining drag them off, jarring over the roots of the survivors, and tumble them into the nearest stream, till, the fairest having fallen, they scamper off to ransack some new wilderness, and all is still again. It is as when a migrating army of mice girdles a forest of pines. The chopper fells trees from the same motive that the mouse gnaws them—to get his living. You tell me that he has a more interesting family than the mouse. That is as it happens. He speaks of a "berth" of timber, a good place for him to get into, just as a worm might.

When the chopper would praise a pine he will commonly tell you that the one he cut was so big that a yoke of oxen stood on its stump; as if that were what the pine had grown for, to become the footstool of oxen. In my mind's eye I can see these unwieldy tame deer, with a yoke binding them together, the brazen-tipped horns betraying their servitude, taking their stand on the stump of each giant pine in succession throughout this whole forest, and chewing their cud there, until it is nothing but an ox-pasture, and run out at that. As if it were good for the oxen, and some medicinal quality ascended into their nostrils. Or is their elevated position intended merely as a symbol of the fact that the pastoral comes next in order to the sylvan or hunter life?

The character of the logger's admiration is betrayed by his very mode of expressing it. If he told all that was in his mind, he would say, "It was so big that I cut it down, and then a yoke of oxen could stand on its stump." He admires the log, the carcass or corpse, more than the tree. Why, my dear sir, the tree might have stood on its own stump, and a great deal more comfortably and firmly than a yoke of oxen can, if you had not cut it down.

The Anglo-American can indeed cut down and grub up all this waving forest, and make a stump speech on its ruins, but he cannot converse with the spirit of the tree he fells, he cannot read the poetry and mythology which retire as he advances. He ignorantly erases mythological tablets in order to print his handbills and town-meeting warrants on them. Before he has learned his a b c in the beautiful but mystic lore of the wilderness he cuts it down, puts up a "deestrict" schoolhouse, and introduces Webster's spelling-book.

Below the last dam, the river being swift and shallow, we two walked about half a mile to lighten the canoe. I made it a rule to carry my knapsack when I walked, and also to keep it tied to a crossbar when in the canoe, that it might be found with the canoe if we should upset.

I heard the dog-day locust here, a sound which I had associated only with more open, if not settled countries.

We were now fairly on the Allegash River. After perhaps two miles of river we entered Heron Lake, scaring up forty or fifty young sheldrakes, at the entrance, which ran over the water with great rapidity, as usual in a long line.

This lake, judging from the map, is about ten miles long. We had entered it on the southwest side, and saw a dark mountain northeast over the lake which the Indian said was called Peaked Mountain, and used by explorers to look for timber from. The shores were in the same ragged and unsightly condition, encumbered with dead timber, both fallen and standing, as in the last lake, owing to the dam on the Allegash below. Some low points or islands were almost drowned.

I saw something white a mile off on the water, which turned out to be a great gull on a rock, which the Indian would have been glad to kill and eat. But it flew away long before we were near; and also a flock of summer ducks that were about the rock with it. I asking him about herons, since this was Heron Lake, he said that he found the blue heron's nests in the hard-wood trees.

Rounding a point, we stood across a bay toward a large island three or four miles down the lake. We met with shadflies midway, about a mile from the shore, and they evidently fly over the whole lake. On Moosehead I had seen a large devil's-needle half a mile from the shore, coming from the middle of the lake, where it was three or four miles wide at least. It had probably crossed.

We landed on the southeast side of the island, which was rather elevated, and densely wooded, with a rocky shore, in season for an early dinner. Somebody had camped there not long before and left the frame on which they stretched a moose-hide. The Indian proceeded at once to cut a canoe birch, slanted it up against another tree on the shore, tying it with a withe, and lay down to sleep in its shade. We made this island the limit of our excursion in this direction.

The next dam was about fifteen miles farther north down the Allegash. We had been told in Bangor of a man who lived alone, a sort of hermit, at that dam, to take care of it, who spent his time tossing a bullet from one hand to the other, for want of employment. This sort of tit-for-tat intercourse between his two hands, bandying to and fro a leaden subject, seems to have been his symbol for society.

There was another island visible toward the north end of the lake, with an elevated clearing on it; but we learned afterward that it was not inhabited, had only been used as a pasture for cattle which summered in these woods. This unnaturally smooth-shaven, squarish spot, in the midst of the otherwise uninterrupted forest, only reminded us how uninhabited the country was. You would sooner expect to meet a bear than an ox in such a clearing. At any rate, it must have been a surprise to the bears when they came across it. Such, seen far or near, you know at once to be man's work, for Nature never does it. In order to let in the light to the earth he clears off the forest on the hillsides and plains, and sprinkles fine grass seed like an enchanter, and so carpets the earth with a firm sward.

Polis had evidently more curiosity respecting the few settlers in those woods than we. If nothing was said, he took it for granted that we wanted to go straight to the next log hut. Having observed that we came by the log huts at Chesuncook, and the blind Canadian's at the Mud Pond carry, without stopping to communicate with the inhabitants, he took occasion now to suggest that the usual way was, when you came near a house, to go to it, and tell the inhabitants what you had seen or heard, and then they told you what they had seen; but we laughed and said that we had had enough of houses for the present, and had come here partly to avoid them.

In the meanwhile, the wind, increasing, blew down the Indian's birch and created such a sea that we found ourselves prisoners on the island, the nearest shore being perhaps a mile distant, and we took the canoe out to prevent its drifting away. We did not know but we should be compelled to spend the rest of the day and the night there. At any rate, the Indian went to sleep again, my companion busied himself drying his plants, and I rambled along the shore westward, which was quite stony, and obstructed with fallen bleached or drifted trees for four or five rods in width.

Our Indian said that he was a doctor, and could tell me some medicinal use for every plant I could show him. I immediately tried him. He said that the inner bark of the aspen was good for sore eyes; and so with various other plants, proving himself as good as his word. According to his account, he had acquired such knowledge in his youth from a wise old Indian with whom he associated, and he lamented that the present generation of Indians "had lost a great deal."

He said that the caribou was a "very great runner," that there were none about this lake now, though there used to be many, and, pointing to the belt of dead trees caused by the dams, he added: "No likum stump. When he sees that he scared."

Pointing southeasterly over the lake and distant forest, he observed, "Me go Oldtown in three days."

I asked how he would get over the swamps and fallen trees. "Oh," said he, "in winter all covered, go anywhere on snowshoes, right across lakes."

What a wilderness walk for a man to take alone! None of your half-mile swamps, none of your mile-wide woods merely, as on the skirts of our towns, without hotels, only a dark mountain or a lake for guide-board and station, over ground much of it impassable in summer!

Here was traveling of the old heroic kind over the unaltered face of nature. From the Allegash River, across great Apmoojenegamook, he takes his way under the bear-haunted slopes of Katahdin to Pamadumcook and Millinocket's inland seas, and so to the forks of the Nicketow, ever pushing the boughs of the fir and spruce aside, with his load of furs, contending day and night, night and day, with the shaggy demon vegetation, traveling through the mossy graveyard of trees. Or he could go by "that rough tooth of the sea" Kineo, great source of arrows and of spears to the ancients, when weapons of stone were used. Seeing and hearing moose, caribou, bears, porcupines, lynxes, wolves, and panthers. Places where he might live and die and never hear of the United States—never hear of America.

There is a lumberer's road called the Eagle Lake Road from the Seboois to the east side of this lake. It may seem strange that any road through such a wilderness should be passable, even in winter, but at that season, wherever lumbering operations are actively carried on, teams are continually passing on the single track, and it becomes as smooth almost as a railway. I am told that in the Aroostook country the sleds are required by law to be of one width, four feet, and sleighs must be altered to fit the track, so that one runner may go in one rut and the other follow the horse. Yet it is very bad turning out.

We had for some time seen a thunder-shower coming up from the west over the woods of the island, and heard the muttering of the thunder, though we were in doubt whether it would reach us; but now the darkness rapidly increasing, and a fresh breeze rustling the forest, we hastily put up the plants which we had been drying, and with one consent made a rush for the tent material and set about pitching it. A place was selected and stakes and pins cut in the shortest possible time, and we were pinning it down lest it should be blown away, when the storm suddenly burst over us.

As we lay huddled together under the tent, which leaked considerably about the sides, with our baggage at our feet, we listened to some of the grandest thunder which I ever heard—rapid peals, round and plump, bang, bang, bang, in succession, like artillery from some fortress in the sky; and the lightning was proportionally brilliant. The Indian said, "It must be good powder." All for the benefit of the moose and us, echoing far over the concealed lakes. I thought it must be a place which the thunder loved, where the lightning practiced to keep its hand in, and it would do no harm to shatter a few pines.

Looking out, I perceived that the violent shower falling on the lake had almost instantaneously flattened the waves, and, it clearing off, we resolved to start immediately, before the wind raised them again.

Getting outside, I said that I saw clouds still in the southwest, and heard thunder there. We embarked, nevertheless, and paddled rapidly back toward the dams.

At the outlet of Chamberlain Lake we were overtaken by another gusty rainstorm, which compelled us to take shelter, the Indian under his canoe on the bank, and we under the edge of the dam. However, we were more scared than wet. From my covert I could see the Indian peeping out from beneath his canoe to see what had become of the rain. When we had taken our respective places thus once or twice, the rain not coming down in earnest, we commenced rambling about the neighborhood, for the wind had by this time raised such waves on the lake that we could not stir, and we feared that we should be obliged to camp there. We got an early supper on the dam and tried for fish, while waiting for the tumult to subside. The fishes were not only few, but small and worthless.

At length, just before sunset, we set out again. It was a wild evening when we coasted up the north side of this Apmoojenegamook Lake. One thunder-storm was just over, and the waves which it had raised still running with violence, and another storm was now seen coming up in the southwest, far over the lake; but it might be worse in the morning, and we wished to get as far as possible on our way while we might.

It blew hard against the shore, which was as dreary and harborless as you can conceive. For half a dozen rods in width it was a perfect maze of submerged trees, all dead and bare and bleaching, some standing half their original height, others prostrate, and criss-across, above or beneath the surface, and mingled with them were loose trees and limbs and stumps, beating about. We could not have landed if we would, without the greatest danger of being swamped; so blow as it might, we must depend on coasting. It was twilight, too, and that stormy cloud was advancing rapidly in our rear. It was a pleasant excitement, yet we were glad to reach, at length, the cleared shore of the Chamberlain Farm.

We landed on a low and thinly wooded point, and while my companions were pitching the tent, I ran up to the house to get some sugar, our six pounds being gone. It was no wonder they were, for Polis had a sweet tooth. He would first fill his dipper nearly a third full of sugar, and then add the coffee to it. Here was a clearing extending back from the lake to a hilltop, with some dark-colored log buildings and a storehouse in it, and half a dozen men standing in front of the principal hut, greedy for news. Among them was the man who tended the dam on the Allegash and tossed the bullet. He, having charge of the dams, and learning that we were going to Webster Stream the next day, told me that some of their men, who were haying at Telos Lake, had shut the dam at the canal there in order to catch trout, and if we wanted more water to take us through the canal we might raise the gate.

They were unwilling to spare more than four pounds of brown sugar,—unlocking the storehouse to get it,— since they only kept a little for such cases as this, and they charged twenty cents a pound for it, which certainly it was worth to get it up there.

When I returned to the shore it was quite dark, but we had a rousing fire to warm and dry us by, and a snug apartment behind it. The Indian went up to the house to inquire after a brother who had been absent hunting a year or two, and while another shower was beginning, I groped about cutting spruce and arbor-vitæ twigs for a bed. I preferred the arbor-vitæ on account of its fragrance, and spread it particularly thick about the shoulders. It is remarkable with what pure satisfaction the traveler in those woods will reach his camping-ground on the eve of a tempestuous night like this, as if he had got to his inn, and, rolling himself in his blanket, stretch himself on his six-feet-by-two bed of dripping fir twigs, with a thin sheet of cotton for roof, snug as a meadow mouse in its nest.

Invariably our best nights were those when it rained, for then we were not troubled with mosquitoes.

You soon come to disregard rain on such excursions, at least in the summer, it is so easy to dry yourself, supposing a dry change of clothing is not to be had. You can much sooner dry you by such a fire as you can make in the woods than in anybody's kitchen, the fireplace is so much larger, and wood so much more abundant. A shed-shaped tent will catch and reflect the heat, and you may be drying while you are sleeping.

Some who have leaky roofs in the towns may have been kept awake, but we were soon lulled asleep by a steady, soaking rain, which lasted all night.

CHAPTER VII

WHEN WE AWOKE it had done raining, though it was still cloudy. The fire was put out, and the Indian's boots, which stood under the eaves of the tent, were half full of water. He was much more improvident in such respects than either of us, and he had to thank us for keeping his powder dry. We decided to cross the lake at once, before breakfast; and before starting I took the bearing of the shore which we wished to strike, about three miles distant, lest a sudden misty rain should conceal it when we were midway.

Though the bay in which we were was perfectly quiet and smooth, we found the lake already wide awake outside, but not dangerously or unpleasantly so. Nevertheless, when you get out on one of those lakes in a canoe like this, you do not forget that you are completely at the mercy of the wind, and a fickle power it is. The playful waves may at any time become too rude for you in their sport, and play right on over you. After much steady paddling and dancing over the dark waves we found ourselves in the neighborhood of the southern land. We breakfasted on a rocky point, the first convenient place that offered.

It was well enough that we crossed thus early, for the waves now ran quite high, but beyond this point we had comparatively smooth water. You can commonly go along one side or the other of a lake, when you cannot cross it.

My companion and I, having a discussion on some point of ancient history, were amused by the attitude which the Indian, who could not tell what we were talking about, assumed. He constituted himself umpire, and, judging by our air and gesture, he very seriously remarked from time to time, "You beat," or "He beat."

Leaving a spacious bay on our left, we entered through a short strait into a small lake a couple of miles over, and thence into Telos Lake. This curved round toward the northeast, and may have been three or four miles long as we paddled.

The outlet from the lake into the East Branch of the Penobscot is an artificial one, and it was not very apparent where it was exactly, but the lake ran curving far up northeasterly into two narrow valleys or ravines, as if it had for a long time been groping its way toward the Penobscot waters. By observing where the horizon was lowest, and following the longest of these, we at length reached the dam, having come about a dozen miles from the last camp. Somebody had left a line set for trout, and the jackknife with which the bait had been cut on the dam beside it, and, on a log close by, a loaf of bread. These proved the property of a solitary hunter, whom we soon met, and canoe and gun and traps were not far off. He told us that it was twenty miles to the foot of Grand Lake, and that the first house below the foot of the lake, on the East Branch, was Hunt's, about forty-five miles farther.

This hunter, who was a quite small, sunburnt man, having already carried his canoe over, had nothing so interesting and pressing to do as to observe our transit. He had been out a month or more alone. How much more respectable is the life of the solitary pioneer or settler in these, or any woods—having real difficulties, not of his own creation, drawing his subsistence directly from nature—than that of the helpless multitudes in the towns who depend on gratifying the extremely artificial wants of society and are thrown out of employment by hard times!

Telos Lake, the head of the St. John on this side, and Webster Pond, the head of the East Branch of the Penobscot, are only about a mile apart, and they are connected by a ravine, in which but little digging was required to make the water of the former, which is the highest, flow into the latter. This canal is something less than a mile long and about four rods wide. The rush of the water has produced such changes in the canal that it has now the appearance of a very rapid mountain stream flowing through a ravine, and you would not suspect that any digging had been required to persuade the waters of the St. John to flow into the Penobscot here. It was so winding that one could see but a little way down.

It is wonderful how well watered this country is. As you paddle across a lake, bays will be pointed out to you, by following up which, and perhaps the tributary stream which empties in, you may, after a short portage, or possibly, at some seasons, none at all, get into another river, which empties far away from the one you are on. Generally, you may go in any direction in a canoe, by making frequent but not very long portages. It seems as if the more youthful and impressionable streams can hardly resist the numerous invitations and temptations to leave their native beds and run down their neighbors' channels.

Wherever there is a channel for water there is a road for the canoe. It is said that some Western steamers can run on a heavy dew, whence we can imagine what a canoe may do.

This canal, so called, was a considerable and extremely rapid and rocky river. The Indian decided that there was water enough in it without raising the dam, which would only make it more violent, and that he would run down it alone, while we carried the greater part of the baggage. Our provisions being about half consumed, there was the less left in the canoe. We had thrown away the pork-keg and wrapped its contents in birch bark.

Following a moist trail through the forest, we reached the head of Webster Pond about the same time with the Indian, notwithstanding the velocity with which he moved, our route being the most direct. The pond was two or three miles long.

At the outlet was another dam, at which we stopped and picked raspberries, while the Indian went down the stream a half-mile through the forest, to see what he had got to contend with. There was a deserted log camp here, apparently used the previous winter, with its "hovel" or barn for cattle. In the hut was a large fir-twig bed, raised two feet from the floor, occupying a large part of the single apartment, a long narrow table against the wall, with a stout log bench before it, and above the table a small window, the only one there was, which admitted a feeble light. It was a simple and strong fort erected against the cold.

We got our dinner on the shore, on the upper side of the dam. As we were sitting by our fire, concealed by the earth bank of the dam, a long line of sheldrakes, half grown, came waddling over it from the water below, passing within about a rod of us, so that we could almost have caught them in our hands. They were very abundant on all the streams and lakes which we visited, and every two or three hours they would rush away in a long string over the water before us, twenty to fifty of them at once, rarely ever flying, but running with great rapidity up or down the stream, even in the midst of the most violent rapids, and apparently as fast up as down.

An Indian at Oldtown had told us that we should be obliged to carry ten miles between Telos Lake on the St. John and Second Lake on the East Branch of the Penobscot; but the lumberers whom we met assured us that there would not be more than a mile of carry. It turned out that the Indian was nearest right, as far as we were concerned. However, if one of us could have assisted the Indian in managing the canoe in the rapids, we might have run the greater part of the way; but as he was alone in the management of the canoe in such places we were obliged to walk the greater part.

My companion and I carried a good part of the baggage on our shoulders, while the Indian took that which would be least injured by wet in the canoe. We did not know when we should see him again, for he had not been this way since the canal was cut. He agreed to stop when he got to smooth water, come up and find our path if he could, and halloo for us, and after waiting a reasonable time go on and try again—and we were to look out in like manner for him.

He commenced by running through the sluiceway and over the dam, as usual, standing up in his tossing canoe, and was soon out of sight behind a point in a wild gorge. This Webster Stream is well known to lumbermen as a difficult one. It is exceedingly rapid and rocky, and also shallow, and can hardly be considered navigable, unless that may mean that what is launched in it is sure to be carried swiftly down it, though it may be dashed to pieces by the way. It is somewhat like navigating a thunder-spout. With commonly an irresistible force urging you on, you have got to choose your own course each moment between the rocks and shallows, and to get into it, moving forward always with the utmost possible moderation, and often holding on, if you can, that you may inspect the rapids before you.

By the Indian's direction we took an old path on the south side, which appeared to keep down the stream. It was a wild wood-path, with a few tracks of oxen which had been driven over it, probably to some old camp clearing for pasturage, mingled with the tracks of moose which had lately used it. We kept on steadily for about an hour without putting down our packs, occasionally winding around or climbing over a fallen tree, for the most part far out of sight and hearing of the river; till, after walking about three miles, we were glad to find that the path came to the river again at an old camp-ground, where there was a small opening in the forest, at which we paused.

Swiftly as the shallow and rocky river ran here, a continuous rapid with dancing waves, I saw, as I sat on the shore, a long string of sheldrakes, which something scared, run up the opposite side of the stream by me, just touching the surface of the waves, and getting an impulse from them as they flowed from under them; but they soon came back, driven by the Indian, who had fallen a little behind us on account of the windings. He shot round a point just above, and came to land by us with considerable water in his canoe. He had found it, as he said, "very strong water," and had been obliged to land once before to empty out what he had taken in.

He complained that it strained him to paddle so hard in order to keep his canoe straight in its course, having no one in the bows to aid him, and, shallow as it was, said that it would be no joke to upset there, for the force of the water was such that he had as lief I would strike him over the head with a paddle as have that water strike him. Seeing him come out of that gap was as if you should pour water down an inclined and zigzag trough, then drop a nutshell into it, and, taking a short cut to the bottom, get there in time to see it come out, notwithstanding the rush and tumult, right side up, and only partly full of water.

After a moment's breathing-space, while I held his canoe, he was soon out of sight again around another bend, and we, shouldering our packs, resumed our course.

Before going a mile we heard the Indian calling to us. He had come up through the woods and along the path to find us, having reached sufficiently smooth water to warrant his taking us in. The shore was about one fourth of a mile distant through a dense, dark forest, and as he led us back to it, winding rapidly about to the right and left, I had the curiosity to look down carefully and found that he was following his steps backward. I could only occasionally perceive his trail in the moss, and yet he did not appear to look down nor hesitate an instant, but led us out exactly to his canoe. This surprised me, for without a compass, or the sight or noise of the river to guide us, we could not have kept our course many minutes, and could have retraced our steps but a short distance, with a great deal of pains and very slowly, using a laborious circumspection. But it was evident that he could go back through the forest wherever he had been during the day.

After this rough walking in the dark woods it was an agreeable change to glide down the rapid river in the canoe once more. This river, though still very swift, was almost perfectly smooth here, and showed a very visible declivity, a regularly inclined plane, for several miles, like a mirror set a little aslant, on which we coasted down. It was very exhilarating, and the perfection of traveling, the coasting down this inclined mirror between two evergreen forests edged with lofty dead white pines, sometimes slanted half-way over the stream. I saw some monsters there, nearly destitute of branches, and scarcely diminishing in diameter for eighty or ninety feet.

As we were thus swept along, our Indian repeated in a deliberate and drawling tone the words, "Daniel Webster, great lawyer," apparently reminded of him by the name of the stream, and he described his calling on him once in Boston at what he supposed was his boarding-house. He had no business with him but merely went to pay his respects, as we should say. It was on the day after Webster delivered his Bunker Hill oration. The first time he called he waited till he was tired without seeing him, and then went away. The next time he saw him go by the door of the room in which he was waiting several times, in his shirt-sleeves, without noticing him. He thought that if he had come to see Indians they would not have treated him so. At length, after very long delay, he came in, walked toward him, and asked in a loud voice, gruffly, "What do you want?" and he, thinking at first, by the motion of his hand, that he was going to strike him, said to himself, "You'd better take care; if you try that I shall know what to do."

He did not like him, and declared that all he said "was not worth talk about a musquash."

Coming to falls and rapids, our easy progress was suddenly terminated. The Indian went alongshore to inspect the water, while we climbed over the rocks, picking berries. When the Indian came back, he remarked, "You got to walk; ver' strong water."

So, taking out his canoe, he launched it again below the falls, and was soon out of sight. At such times he would step into the canoe, take up his paddle, and start off, looking far down-stream as if absorbing all the intelligence of forest and stream into himself. We meanwhile scrambled along the shore with our packs, without any path. This was the last of *our* boating for the day.

The Indian now got along much faster than we, and waited for us from time to time. I found here the only cool spring that I drank at anywhere on this excursion, a little water filling a hollow in the sandy bank. It was a quite memorable event, and due to the elevation of the country, for wherever else we had been the water in the rivers and the streams emptying in was dead and warm, compared with that of a mountainous region. It was very bad walking along the shore over fallen and drifted trees and bushes, and rocks, from time to time swinging ourselves round over the water, or else taking to a gravel bar or going inland. At one place, the Indian being ahead, I was obliged to take off all my clothes in order to ford a small but deep stream emptying in, while my companion, who was inland, found a rude bridge, high up in the woods, and I saw no more of him for some time. I saw there very fresh moose tracks, and I passed one white pine log, lodged in the forest near the edge of the stream, which was quite five feet in diameter at the butt.

Shortly after this I overtook the Indian at the edge of some burnt land, which extended three or four miles at least, beginning about three miles above Second Lake, which we were expecting to reach that night. This burnt region was still more rocky than before, but, though comparatively open, we could not yet see the lake. Not having seen my companion for some time, I climbed with the Indian a high rock on the edge of the river forming a narrow ridge only a foot or two wide at top, in order to look for him. After calling many times I at length heard him answer from a considerable distance inland, he having taken a trail which led off from the river, and being now in search of the river again. Seeing a much higher rock of the same character about one third of a mile farther down-stream, I proceeded toward it through the burnt land, in order to look for the lake from its summit, and hallooing all the while that my companion might join me on the way.

Before we came together I noticed where a moose, which possibly I had scared by my shouting, had apparently

just run along a large rotten trunk of a pine, which made
a bridge thirty or forty feet long over a hollow, as convenient for him as for me. The tracks were as large as those
of an ox, but an ox could not have crossed there. This
burnt land was an exceedingly wild and desolate region.
Judging by the weeds and sprouts, it appeared to have
been burnt about two years before. It was covered with
charred trunks, either prostrate or standing, which crocked
our clothes and hands. Great shells of trees, sometimes
unburnt without, or burnt on one side only, but black
within, stood twenty or forty feet high. The fire had run
up inside, as in a chimney, leaving the sapwood. There
were great fields of fireweed, which presented masses of
pink. Intermixed with these were blueberry and raspberry
bushes.

Having crossed a second rocky ridge, when I was beginning to ascend the third, the Indian, whom I had left on
the shore, beckoned to me to come to him, but I made
sign that I would first ascend the rock before me. My
companion accompanied me to the top.

There was a remarkable series of these great rock-waves
revealed by the burning; breakers, as it were. No wonder
that the river that found its way through them was rapid
and obstructed by falls. We could see the lake over the
woods, and that the river made an abrupt turn southward
around the end of the cliff on which we stood, and that
there was an important fall in it a short distance below
us. I could see the canoe a hundred rods behind, but now
on the opposite shore, and supposed that the Indian had
concluded to take out and carry round some bad rapids
on that side, but after waiting a while I could still see

nothing of him, and I began to suspect that he had gone inland to look for the lake from some hilltop on that side. This proved to be the case, for after I had started to return to the canoe I heard a faint halloo, and descried him on the top of a distant rocky hill. I began to return along the ridge toward the angle in the river. My companion inquired where I was going; to which I answered that I was going far enough back to communicate with the Indian.

When we reached the shore the Indian appeared from out the woods on the opposite side, but on account of the roar of the water it was difficult to communicate with him. He kept along the shore westward to his canoe, while we stopped at the angle where the stream turned south-ward around the precipice. I said to my companion that we would keep along the shore and keep the Indian in sight. We started to do so, being close together, the Indian behind us having launched his canoe again, but I saw the latter beckoning to me, and I called to my companion, who had just disappeared behind large rocks at the point of the precipice on his way down the stream, that I was going to help the Indian.

I did so—helped get the canoe over a fall, lying with my breast over a rock, and holding one end while he received it below—and within ten or fifteen minutes I was back at the point where the river turned southward, while Polis glided down the river alone, parallel with me. But to my surprise, when I rounded the precipice, though the shore was bare of trees, without rocks, for a quarter of a mile at least, my companion was not to be seen. It was as if he had sunk into the earth. This was the more unaccountable to me, because I knew that his feet were very sore, and that he wished to keep with the party.

I hastened along, hallooing and searching for him, thinking he might be concealed behind a rock, but the Indian had got along faster in his canoe, till he was arrested by the falls, about a quarter of a mile below. He then landed, and said that we could go no farther that night. The sun was setting, and on account of falls and rapids we should be obliged to leave this river and carry a good way into another farther east. The first thing then was to find my companion, for I was now very much alarmed about him, and I sent the Indian along the shore downstream, which began to be covered with unburnt wood again just below the falls, while I searched backward about the precipice which we had passed.

The Indian showed some unwillingness to exert himself, complaining that he was very tired in consequence of his day's work, that it had strained him getting down so many rapids alone; but he went off calling somewhat like an owl. I remembered that my companion was nearsighted, and I feared that he had either fallen from the precipice, or fainted and sunk down amid the rocks beneath it. I shouted and searched above and below this precipice in the twilight till I could not see, expecting nothing less than to find his body beneath it. For half an hour I anticipated and believed only the worst. I thought what I should do the next day if I did not find him, and how his relatives would feel if I should return without him. I felt that if he were really lost away from the river there, it would be a desperate undertaking to find him; and where were they who could help you? What would it be to raise the country, where there were only two or three camps, twenty or thirty miles apart, and no road, and perhaps nobody at home?

I rushed down from this precipice to the canoe in order to fire the Indian's gun, but found that my companion had the caps. When the Indian returned he said that he had seen his tracks once or twice along the shore. This encouraged me very much. He objected to firing the gun, saying that if my companion heard it, which was not likely, on account of the roar of the stream, it would tempt him to come toward us, and he might break his neck in the dark. For the same reason we refrained from lighting a fire on the highest rock. I proposed that we should both keep down the stream to the lake, or that I should go at any rate, but the Indian said: "No use, can't do anything in the dark. Come morning, then we find 'em. No harm— he make 'em camp. No bad animals here—warm night—he well off as you and I."

The darkness in the woods was by this so thick that it decided the question. We must camp where we were. I knew that he had his knapsack, with blankets and matches, and, if well, would fare no worse than we, except that he would have no supper nor society.

This side of the river being so encumbered with rocks, we crossed to the eastern or smoother shore, and proceeded to camp there, within two or three rods of the falls. We pitched no tent, but lay on the sand, putting a few handfuls of grass and twigs under us, there being no evergreen at hand. For fuel we had some of the charred stumps. Our various bags of provisions had got quite wet in the rapids, and I arranged them about the fire to dry. The fall close by was the principal one on this stream, and it shook the earth under us. It was a cool, dewy night. I lay awake a good deal from anxiety. From time to time I fancied that I heard his voice calling through the roar of the falls from the opposite side of the river; but it is doubtful if we could have heard him across the stream there. Sometimes I doubted whether the Indian had really seen his tracks, since he manifested an unwillingness to make much of a search.

It was the most wild and desolate region we had camped in, where, if anywhere, one might expect to meet with befitting inhabitants, but I heard only the squeak of a nighthawk flitting over. The moon in her first quarter, in the fore part of the night, setting over the bare rocky hills garnished with tall, charred, and hollow stumps or shells of trees, served to reveal the desolation.

CHAPTER VIII

Thursday, July 30

I AROUSED THE Indian early to go in search of our companion, expecting to find him within a mile or two, farther down the stream. The Indian wanted his breakfast first, but I reminded him that my companion had had neither breakfast nor supper. We were obliged first to carry our canoe and baggage over into another stream, the main East Branch, about three fourths of a mile distant, for Webster Stream was no farther navigable. We went twice over this carry, and the dewy bushes wet us through like water up to the middle. I hallooed from time to time, though I had little expectation that I could be heard over the roar of the rapids.

In going over this portage the last time, the Indian, who was before me with the canoe on his head, stumbled and fell heavily once, and lay for a moment silent as if in pain. I hastily stepped forward to help him, asking if he was much hurt, but after a moment's pause, without replying, he sprang up and went forward.

We had launched our canoe and gone but little way down the East Branch, when I heard an answering shout from my companion, and soon after saw him standing on a point where there was a clearing a quarter of a mile below, and the smoke of his fire was rising near by. Before I saw him I naturally shouted again and again, but the Indian curtly remarked, "He hears you," as if once was enough.

It was just below the mouth of Webster Stream. When
we arrived he was smoking his pipe, and said that he had
passed a pretty comfortable night, though it was rather
cold, on account of the dew. It appeared that when we
stood together the previous evening, and I was shouting
to the Indian across the river, he, being nearsighted, had
not seen the Indian nor his canoe, and when I went back
to the Indian's assistance, did not see which way I went,
and supposed that we were below and not above him,
and so, making haste to catch up, he ran away from us.
Having reached this clearing, a mile or more below our
camp, the night overtook him, and he made a fire in a
little hollow, and lay down by it in his blanket, still thinking
that we were ahead of him.

He had stuck up the remnant of a lumberer's shirt, found
on the point, on a pole by the waterside for a signal, and
attached a note to it to inform us that he had gone on to
the lake, and that if he did not find us there he would be
back in a couple of hours. If he had not found us soon he
had some thoughts of going back in search of the solitary
hunter whom we had met at Telos Lake, ten miles behind,
and, if successful, hire him to take him to Bangor. But if
this hunter had moved as fast as we, he would have been
twenty miles off by this time, and who could guess in what
direction? It would have been like looking for a needle in
a haymow to search for him in these woods. He had been
considering how long he could live on berries alone.

We all had good appetites for the breakfast which we
made haste to cook here, and then, having partially dried
our clothes, we glided swiftly down the winding stream
toward Second Lake.

As the shores became flatter with frequent sandbars, and the stream more winding in the lower land near the lake, elms and ash trees made their appearance; also the wild yellow lily, some of whose bulbs I collected for a soup. On some ridges the burnt land extended as far as the lake. This was a very beautiful lake, two or three miles long, with high mountains on the southwest side. The morning was a bright one, and perfectly still, the lake as smooth as glass, we making the only ripple as we paddled into it. The dark mountains about it were seen through a glaucous mist, and the white stems of canoe birches mingled with the other woods around it. The thrush sang on the distant shore, and the laugh of some loons, sporting in a concealed western bay, as if inspired by the morning, came distinct over the lake to us. The beauty of the scene may have been enhanced to our eyes by the fact that we had just come together after a night of some anxiety.

Having paddled down three quarters of the lake, we came to a standstill while my companion let down for fish. In the midst of our dreams of giant lake trout, even then supposed to be nibbling, our fisherman drew up a diminutive red perch, and we took up our paddles.

It was not apparent where the outlet of the lake was, and while the Indian thought it was in one direction, I thought it was in another. He said, "I bet you fourpence it is there," but he still held on in my direction, which proved to be the right one.

As we were approaching the outlet he suddenly exclaimed, "Moose! moose!" and told us to be still. He put a cap on his gun, and, standing up in the stern, rapidly pushed the canoe straight toward the shore and the moose. It was a cow moose, about thirty rods off, standing in the water by the side of the outlet, partly behind some fallen timber and bushes, and at that distance she did not look very large. She was flapping her large ears, and from time to time poking off the flies with her nose from some part of her body. She did not appear much alarmed by our neighborhood, only occasionally turned her head and looked straight at us, and then gave her attention to the flies again. As we approached nearer she got out of the water, stood higher, and regarded us more suspiciously.

Polis pushed the canoe steadily forward in the shallow water, but the canoe soon grounded in the mud eight or ten rods distant from the moose, and the Indian seized his gun. After standing still a moment she turned so as to expose her side, and he improved this moment to fire, over our heads. She thereupon moved off eight or ten rods at a moderate pace across a shallow bay to the opposite shore, and she stood still again while the Indian hastily loaded and fired twice at her, without her moving. My companion, who passed him his caps and bullets, said that Polis was as excited as a boy of fifteen, that his hand trembled, and he once put his ramrod back upside down.

The Indian now pushed quickly and quietly back, and a long distance round, in order to get into the outlet,—for he had fired over the neck of a peninsula between it and the lake,—till we approached the place where the moose had stood, when he exclaimed, "She is a goner!"

There, to be sure, she lay perfectly dead, just where she had stood to receive the last shots. Using a tape, I found that the moose measured six feet from the shoulder to the tip of the hoof, and was eight feet long.

Polis, preparing to skin the moose, asked me to help him find a stone on which to sharpen his large knife. It being flat alluvial ground, covered with red maples, etc., this was no easy matter. We searched far and wide a long time till at length I found a flat kind of slate stone, on which he soon made his knife very sharp.

While he was skinning the moose I proceeded to ascertain what kind of fishes were to be found in the sluggish and muddy outlet. The greatest difficulty was to find a pole. It was almost impossible to find a slender, straight pole ten or twelve feet long in those woods. You might search half an hour in vain. They are commonly spruce, arbor-vitæ, fir, etc., short, stout, and branchy, and do not make good fishpoles, even after you have patiently cut off all their tough and scraggy branches. The fishes were red perch and chivin.

The Indian, having cut off a large piece of sirloin, the upper lip, and the tongue, wrapped them in the hide, and placed them in the bottom of the canoe, observing that there was "one man," meaning the weight of one. Our load had previously been reduced some thirty pounds, but a hundred pounds were now added, which made our quarters still more narrow, and considerably increased the danger on the lakes and rapids as well as the labor of the carries. The skin was ours according to custom, since the Indian was in our employ, but we did not think of claiming it. He being a skillful dresser of moose-hides would make it worth seven or eight dollars to him, as I was told. He said that he sometimes earned fifty or sixty dollars in a day at them; he had killed ten moose in one day, though the skinning and all took two days. This was the way he had got his property.

We continued along the outlet through a swampy region, by a long, winding deadwater, very much choked up by wood, where we were obliged to land sometimes in order to get the canoe over a log. It was hard to find any channel, and we did not know but we should be lost in the swamp. It abounded in ducks, as usual. At length we reached Grand Lake.

We stopped to dine on an interesting rocky island, securing our canoe to the cliffy shore. Here was a good opportunity to dry our dewy blankets on the open sunny rock. Indians had recently camped here, and accidentally burned over the western end of the island. Polis picked up a gun-case of blue broadcloth, and said that he knew the Indian it belonged to and would carry it to him. His tribe is not so large but he may know all its effects. We proceeded to make a fire and cook our dinner amid some pines.

I saw where the Indians had made canoes in a little secluded hollow in the woods, on the top of the rock, where they were out of the wind, and large piles of whittlings remained. This must have been a favorite resort of their ancestors, and, indeed, we found here the point of an arrow-head, such as they have not used for two centuries and now know not how to make. The Indian picked up a yellowish curved bone by the side of our fireplace and asked me to guess what it was. It was one of the upper incisors of a beaver, on which some party had feasted within a year or two. I found also most of the teeth and the skull. We here dined on fried moose meat.

Our blankets being dry, we set out again, the Indian, as usual, having left his gazette on a tree. We paddled southward, keeping near the western shore. The Indian did not know exactly where the outlet was, and he went feeling his way by a middle course between two probable points, from which he could diverge either way at last without losing much distance. In approaching the south shore, as the clouds looked gusty and the waves ran pretty high, we so steered as to get partly under the lee of an island, though at a great distance from it.

I could not distinguish the outlet till we were almost in it, and heard the water falling over the dam there. Here was a considerable fall, and a very substantial dam, but no sign of a cabin or camp.

While we loitered here Polis took occasion to cut with his big knife some of the hair from his moose-hide, and so lightened and prepared it for drying. I noticed at several old Indian camps in the woods the pile of hair which they had cut from their hides.

Having carried over the dam, he darted down the rapids, leaving us to walk for a mile or more, where for the most part there was no path, but very thick and difficult traveling near the stream. He would call to let us know where he was waiting for us with his canoe, when, on account of the windings of the stream, we did not know where the shore was, but he did not call often enough, forgetting that we were not Indians. He seemed to be very saving of his breath—yet he would be surprised if we went by, or did not strike the right spot. This was not because he was unaccommodating, but a proof of superior manners. Indians like to get along with the least possible communication and ado. He was really paying us a great compliment all the while, thinking that we preferred a hint to a kick.

At length, climbing over the willows and fallen trees, when this was easier than to go round or under them, we overtook the canoe, and glided down the stream in smooth but swift water for several miles. I here observed, as at Webster Stream, that the river was a smooth and regularly inclined plane down which we coasted.

We decided to camp early that we might have ample time before dark. So we stopped at the first favorable shore, where there was a narrow gravelly beach, some five miles below the outlet of the lake. Two steps from the water on either side, and you come to the abrupt, bushy, and rooty, if not turfy, edge of the bank, four or five feet high, where the interminable forest begins, as if the stream had but just cut its way through it.

It is surprising on stepping ashore anywhere into this unbroken wilderness to see so often, at least within a few rods of the river, the marks of the axe, made by lumberers who have either camped here or driven logs past in previous springs. You will see perchance where they have cut large chips from a tall white pine stump for their fire.

While we were pitching the camp and getting supper, the Indian cut the rest of the hair from his moose-hide, and proceeded to extend it vertically on a temporary frame between two small trees, half a dozen feet from the opposite side of the fire, lashing and stretching it with arbor-vitæ bark. Asking for a new kind of tea, he made us some pretty good of the checkerberry, which covered the ground, dropping a little bunch of it tied up with cedar bark into the kettle.

After supper he put on the moose tongue and lips to boil. He showed me how to write on the under side of birch bark with a black spruce twig, which is hard and tough and can be brought to a point.

The Indian wandered off into the woods a short distance just before night, and, coming back, said, "Me found great treasure."

"What's that?" we asked.

"Steel traps, under a log, thirty or forty, I didn't count 'em. I guess Indian work—worth three dollars apiece."

It was a singular coincidence that he should have chanced to walk to and look under that particular log in that trackless forest.

I saw chivin and chub in the stream when washing my hands, but my companion tried in vain to catch them. I heard the sound of bullfrogs from a swamp on the opposite side.

You commonly make your camp just at sundown, and are collecting wood, getting your supper, or pitching your tent while the shades of night are gathering around and adding to the already dense gloom of the forest. You have no time to explore or look around you before it is dark. You may penetrate half a dozen rods farther into that twilight wilderness after some dry bark to kindle your fire with, and wonder what mysteries lie hidden still deeper in it, or you may run down to the shore for a dipper of water, and get a clearer view for a short distance up or down the stream, and while you stand there, see a fish leap, or duck alight in the river, or hear a thrush or robin sing in the woods.

But there is no sauntering off to see the country. Ten or fifteen rods seems a great way from your companions, and you come back with the air of a much traveled man, as from a long journey, with adventures to relate, though you may have heard the crackling of the fire all the while—and at a hundred rods you might be lost past recovery and have to camp out. It is all mossy and *moosey*. In some of those dense fir and spruce woods there is hardly room for the smoke to go up. The trees are a *standing* night, and every fir and spruce which you fell is a plume plucked from night's raven wing. Then at night the general stillness is more impressive than any sound, but occasionally you hear the note of an owl farther or nearer in the woods, and if near a lake, the semihuman cry of the loons at their unearthly revels.

To-night the Indian lay between the fire and his stretched moose-hide, to avoid mosquitoes. Indeed, he also made a small smoky fire of damp leaves at his head and feet, and then as usual rolled up his head in his blanket. We with our veils and our wash were tolerably comfortable, but it would be difficult to pursue any sedentary occupation in the woods at this season; you cannot see to read much by the light of a fire through a veil in the evening, nor handle pencil and paper well with gloves or anointed fingers.

CHAPTER IX

Friday, July 31

WE HAD SMOOTH but swift water for a considerable distance, where we glided rapidly along, scaring up ducks and kingfishers. But, as usual, our smooth progress ere long come to an end, and we were obliged to carry canoe and all about half a mile down the right bank around some rapids or falls. It required sharp eyes sometimes to tell which side was the carry, before you went over the falls, but Polis never failed to land us rightly. The raspberries were particularly abundant and large here, and all hands went to eating them, the Indian remarking on their size.

Often on bare rocky carries the trail was so indistinct that I repeatedly lost it, but when I walked behind him I observed that he could keep it almost like a hound, and rarely hesitated, or, if he paused a moment on a bare rock, his eye immediately detected some sign which would have escaped me. Frequently *we* found no path at all at these places, and were to him unaccountably delayed. He would only say it was "ver' strange."

We had heard of a Grand Fall on this stream, and thought that each fall we came to must be it, but after christening several in succession with this name we gave up the search. There were more Grand or Petty Falls than I can remember.

I cannot tell how many times we had to walk on account of falls or rapids. We were expecting all the while

that the river would take a final leap and get to smooth
water, but there was no improvement this forenoon.
However, the carries were an agreeable variety. So surely
as we stepped out of the canoe and stretched our legs we
found ourselves in a blueberry and raspberry garden, each
side of our rocky trail being lined with one or both. There
was not a carry on the main East Branch where we did
not find an abundance of both these berries, for these
were the rockiest places and partially cleared, such as these
plants prefer, and there had been none to gather the finest
before us.

We bathed and dined at the foot of one of these carries.
It was the Indian who commonly reminded us that it was
dinner-time, sometimes even by turning the prow to the
shore. He once made an indirect, but lengthy apology, by
saying that we might think it strange, but that one who
worked hard all day was very particular to have his dinner
in good season. At the most considerable fall on this stream,
when I was walking over the carry close behind the Indian,
he observed a track on the rock, which was but slightly
covered with soil, and, stooping, muttered, "Caribou."

When we returned, he observed a much larger track
near the same place, where some animal's foot had sunk
into a small hollow in the rock, partly filled with grass
and earth, and he exclaimed with surprise, "What that?"

"Well, what is it?" I asked.

Stooping and laying his hand in it, he answered with
a mysterious air, and in a half-whisper, "Devil—ledges
about here—very bad animal—pull 'em rocks all to pieces."

"How long since it was made?" I asked.

"To-day or yesterday," said he.

We spent at least half the time in walking to-day. The Indian, being alone, commonly ran down far below the foot of the carries before he waited for us. The carry-paths themselves were more than usually indistinct, often the route being revealed only by the countless small holes in the fallen timber made by the tacks in the drivers' boots. It was a tangled and perplexing thicket, through which we stumbled and threaded our way, and when we had finished a mile of it, our starting-point seemed far away. We were glad that we had not got to walk to Bangor along the banks of this river, which would be a journey of more than a hundred miles. Think of the denseness of the forest, the fallen trees and rocks, the windings of the river, the streams emptying in, and the frequent swamps to be crossed. It made you shudder. Yet the Indian from time to time pointed out to us where he had thus crept along day after day when he was a boy of ten, and in a starving condition.

He had been hunting far north of this with two grown Indians. The winter came on unexpectedly early, and the ice compelled them to leave their canoe at Grand Lake, and walk down the bank. They shouldered their furs and started for Oldtown. The snow was not deep enough for snowshoes, or to cover the inequalities of the ground. Polis was soon too weak to carry any burden, but he managed to catch one otter. This was the most they all had to eat on this journey, and he remembered how good the yellow lily roots were, made into a soup with the otter oil. He shared this food equally with the other two, but being so small he suffered much more than they. He waded through the Mattawamkeag at its mouth, when it was freezing cold and came up to his chin, and he, being very weak and emaciated, expected to be swept away. The first house which they reached was at Lincoln, and thereabouts they met a white teamster with supplies, who, seeing their condition, gave them as much as they could eat. For six months after getting home he was very low and did not expect to live, and was perhaps always the worse for it.

For seven or eight miles below that succession of "Grand" falls the aspect of the banks as well as the character of the stream was changed. After passing a tributary from the northeast we had swift smooth water. Low grassy banks and muddy shores began. Many elms as well as maples and more ash trees overhung the stream and supplanted the spruce.

Mosquitoes, black flies, etc., pursued us in mid-channel, and we were glad sometimes to get into violent rapids, for then we escaped them. As we glided swiftly down the inclined plane of the river, a great cat owl launched itself away from a stump on the bank, and flew heavily across the stream, and the Indian, as usual, imitated its note. Soon afterward a white-headed eagle sailed down the stream before us. We drove him several miles, while we were looking for a good place to camp,—for we expected to be overtaken by a shower,—and still we could distinguish him by his white tail, sailing away from time to time from some tree by the shore still farther down the stream. Some *she-corways* being surprised by us, a part of them dived, and we passed directly over them, and could trace their course here and there by a bubble on the surface, but we did not see them come up.

It was some time before we found a camping-place, for the shore was either too grassy and muddy, where mosquitoes abounded, or too steep a hillside. We at length found a place to our minds, where, in a very dense spruce wood above a gravelly shore, there seemed to be but few insects. The trees were so thick that we were obliged to clear a space to build our fire and lie down in, and the young spruce trees that were left were like the wall of an apartment rising around us. We were obliged to pull ourselves up a steep bank to get there. But the place which you have selected for your camp, though never so rough and grim, begins at once to have its attractions, and becomes a very center of civilization to you: "Home is home, be it never so homely."

The mosquitoes were numerous, and the Indian complained a good deal, though he lay, as the night before, between three fires and his stretched hide. As I sat on a stump by the fire with a veil and gloves on, trying to read, he observed, "I make you candle," and in a minute he took a piece of birch bark about two inches wide and rolled it hard, like an allumette★ fifteen inches long, lit it, fixed it by the other end horizontally in a split stick three feet high, and stuck it in the ground, turning the blazing end to the wind, and telling me to snuff it from time to time. It answered the purpose of a candle pretty well.

I noticed, as I had before, that there was a lull among the mosquitoes about midnight, and that they began again in the morning. Apparently they need rest as well as we. Few, if any, creatures are equally active all night. As soon as it was light I saw, through my veil, that the inside of

---

★ A match. In this case an old-fashioned "spill," or lamplighter, made by twisting a piece of paper, into a long, tight spiral roll.

the tent about our heads was quite blackened with myriads, and their combined hum was almost as bad to endure as their stings. I had an uncomfortable night on this account, though I am not sure that one succeeded in his attempt to sting me.

❧ CHAPTER X ☙

Saturday, Sunday, Monday August 1–3

I CAUGHT TWO or three large red chivin within twenty feet of the camp, which, added to the moose tongue that had been left in the kettle boiling over night, and to our other stores, made a sumptuous breakfast. The Indian made us some hemlock tea instead of coffee. This was tolerable, though he said it was not strong enough. It was interesting to see so simple a dish as a kettle of water with a handful of green hemlock sprigs in it boiling over the huge fire in the open air, the leaves fast losing their lively green color, and know that it was for our breakfast.

We were glad to embark once more and leave some of the mosquitoes behind. We found that we had camped about a mile above Hunt's, which is the last house for those who ascend Katahdin on this side. We had expected to ascend it from this point, but my companion was obliged to give up this on account of sore feet. The Indian, however, suggested that perhaps he might get a pair of moccasins at this place, and that he could walk very easily in them without hurting his feet, wearing several pairs of stockings, and he said beside that they were so porous that when you had taken in water it all drained out in a little while. We stopped to get some sugar, but found that the family had moved away, and the house was unoccupied, except temporarily by some men who were getting the hay. I noticed a seine here stretched on the bank, which probably had been used to catch salmon.

Just below this, on the west bank, we saw a moose-hide stretched, and with it a bearskin. The Indian said they belonged to Joe Aitteon,★ but how he told I do not know. He was probably hunting near and had left them for the day. Finding that we were going directly to Oldtown, he regretted that he had not taken more of the moose meat to his family, saying that in a short time, by drying it, he could have made it so light as to have brought away the greater part, leaving the bones. We once or twice inquired after the lip, which is a famous tidbit, but he said, "That go Oldtown for my old woman; don't get it every day."

Maples grew more and more numerous. It rained a little during the forenoon, and, as we expected a wetting, we stopped early and dined just above Whetstone Falls, about a dozen miles below Hunt's. My companion, having lost his pipe, asked the Indian if he could make him one.

"Oh, yer," said he, and in a minute rolled up one of birch bark, telling him to wet the bowl from time to time.

We carried round the falls. The distance was about three fourths of a mile. When we had carried over one load, the Indian returned by the shore, and I by the path; and though I made no particular haste I was nevertheless surprised to find him at the other end as soon as I. It was remarkable how easily he got over the worst ground. He

---

★ Joe Aitteon was Thoreau's guide on the second of his three excursions into the Maine Woods. He was an Indian whose home was on the same island where Polis lived.

said to me, "I take canoe and you take the rest, suppose you can keep along with me?"

I thought he meant that while he ran down the rapids I should keep along the shore, and be ready to assist him from time to time, as I had done before; but as the walking would be very bad, I answered, "I suppose you will go too fast for me, but I will try."

But I was to go by the path, he said. This I thought would not help the matter, I should have so far to go to get to the riverside when he wanted me. But neither was this what he meant. He was proposing a race over the carry, and asked me if I thought I could keep along with him by the same path, adding that I must be pretty smart to do it. As his load, the canoe, would be much the heaviest and bulkiest, I thought that I ought to be able to do it, and said that I would try. So I proceeded to gather up the gun, axe, paddle, kettle, frying-pan, plates, dippers, carpets, etc., and while I was thus engaged he threw me his cowhide boots. "What, are these in the bargain?" I asked.

"Oh, yer," said he; but before I could make a bundle of my load I saw him disappearing over a hill with the canoe on his head.

Hastily scraping the various articles together, I started on the run, and immediately went by him in the bushes, but I had no sooner left him out of sight in a rocky hollow than the greasy plates, dippers, etc., took to themselves wings, and while I was employed in gathering them up, he went by me; but, hastily pressing the sooty kettle to my side, I started once more, and, soon passing him again, I saw him no more on the carry. I do not mention this as anything of a feat, for it was but poor running on my part, and he was obliged to move with great caution for fear of breaking his canoe as well as his neck. When he made his appearance, puffing and panting like myself, in answer to my inquiries where he had been, he said, "Locks cut 'em feet," and, laughing, added, "Oh, me love to play sometimes."

He said that he and his companions when they came to carries several miles long used to try who would get over first; each perhaps with a canoe on his head. I bore the sign of the kettle on my brown linen sack for the rest of the voyage.

As we approached the mouth of the East Branch we passed two or three huts, the first sign of civilization after Hunt's, though we saw no road as yet. We heard a cowbell, and even saw an infant held up to a small square window to see us pass. On entering the West Branch at Nicketow, Polis remarked that it was all smooth water hence to Oldtown, and he threw away his pole which was cut on the Umbazookskus.

We camped about two miles below Nicketow, covering with fresh twigs the withered bed of a former traveler, and feeling that we were now in a settled country, especially when in the evening we heard an ox sneeze in its wild pasture across the river. Wherever you land along the frequented part of the river you have not far to go to find these sites of temporary inns, the withered bed of flattened twigs, the charred sticks, and perhaps the tent-poles. Not long since, similar beds were spread along the Connecticut, the Hudson, and the Delaware, and longer still ago, by the Thames and Seine, and they now help to make the soil where private and public gardens, mansions, and palaces are. We could not get fir twigs for our bed here, and the spruce was harsh in comparison, having more twig in proportion to its leaf, but we improved it somewhat with hemlock.

After the regular supper we attempted to make a lily soup of the bulbs which I had brought along, for I wished to learn all I could before I got out of the woods. Following the Indian's directions, I washed the bulbs carefully, minced some moose meat and some pork, salted and boiled all together, but we had not the patience to try the experiment fairly, for he said it must be boiled till the roots were completely softened so as to thicken the soup like flour; but though we left it on all night, we found it dried to the kettle in the morning and not yet boiled to a flour. Perhaps the roots were not ripe enough, for they commonly gather them in the fall. The Indian's name for these bulbs was *sheepnoc*.

He prepared to camp as usual between his moose-hide and the fire, but it beginning to rain suddenly he took refuge under the tent with us, and gave us a song before falling asleep. It rained hard in the night and spoiled another box of matches for us, which the Indian had left out, for he was very careless; but we had so much the better night for the rain, since it kept the mosquitoes down.

Sunday, a cloudy and unpromising morning. One of us observed to the Indian, "You did not stretch your moose-hide last night, did you, Mr. Polis?"

Whereat he replied in a tone of surprise, though perhaps not of ill humor: "What you ask me that question for?

Suppose I stretch 'em, you see 'em. May be your way talking, may be all right, no Indian way."

I had observed that he did not wish to answer the same question more than once, and was often silent when it was put again, as if he were moody. Not that he was incommunicative, for he frequently commenced a long-winded narrative of his own accord—repeated at length the tradition of some old battle, or some passage in the recent history of his tribe in which he had acted a prominent part, from time to time drawing a long breath, and resuming the thread of his tale, with the true story-teller's leisureliness. Especially after the day's work was over, and he had put himself in posture for the night, he would be unexpectedly sociable, and we would fall asleep before he got through.

The Indian was quite sick this morning with the colic. I thought that he was the worse for the moose meat he had eaten.

We reached the Mattawamkeag at half past eight in the morning, in the midst of a drizzling rain, and, after buying some sugar, set out again.

The Indian growing much worse, we stopped in the north part of Lincoln to get some brandy for him, but, failing in this, an apothecary recommended Brandreth's pills, which he refused to take because he was not acquainted with them. He said, "Me doctor—first study my case, find out what ail 'em—then I know what to take."

We stopped at mid-forenoon on an island and made him a dipper of tea. Here, too, we dined and did some washing and botanizing, while he lay on the bank. In the afternoon we went on a little farther. As a thunder-shower appeared to be coming up we stopped opposite a barn on the west bank. Here we were obliged to spend the rest of the day and night, on account of our patient, whose sickness did not abate. He lay groaning under his canoe on the bank, looking very woebegone. You would not have thought, if you had seen him lying about thus, that he was worth six thousand dollars and had been to Washington. It seemed to me that he made a greater ado about his sickness than a Yankee does, and was more alarmed about himself. We talked somewhat of leaving him with his people in Lincoln,—for that is one of their homes,—but he objected on account of the expense, saying, "Suppose me well in morning, you and I go Oldtown by noon."

As we were taking our tea at twilight, while he lay groaning under his canoe, he asked me to get him a dipper of water. Taking the dipper in one hand, he seized his powderhorn with the other, and, pouring into it a charge or two of powder, stirred it up with his finger, and drank it off. This was all he took to-day after breakfast beside his tea.

To save the trouble of pitching our tent, when we had secured our stores from wandering dogs, we camped in the solitary half-open barn near the bank, with the permission of the owner, lying on new-mown hay four feet deep. The fragrance of the hay, in which many ferns, etc., were mingled, was agreeable, though it was quite alive with grasshoppers which you could hear crawling through it. This served to graduate our approach to houses and feather beds. In the night some large bird, probably an owl, flitted through over our heads, and very early in the morning we were awakened by the twittering of swallows which had their nests there.

We started early before breakfast, the Indian being considerably better, and soon glided by Lincoln, and stopped to breakfast two or three miles below this town.

We frequently passed Indian islands with their small houses on them. The Penobscot Indians seem to be more social even than the whites. Ever and anon in the deepest wilderness of Maine you come to the log hut of a Yankee or Canada settler, but a Penobscot never takes up his residence in such a solitude. They are not even scattered about on their islands in the Penobscot, but gathered together on two or three, evidently for the sake of society. I saw one or two houses not now used by them, because, as our Indian said, they were too solitary.

From time to time we met Indians in their canoes going up river. Our man did not commonly approach them, but only exchanged a few words with them at a distance. We took less notice of the scenery to-day, because we were in quite a settled country. The river became broad and sluggish, and we saw a blue heron winging its way slowly down the stream before us.

The Sunkhaze, a short dead stream, comes in from the east two miles above Oldtown. Asking the meaning of this name, the Indian said, "Suppose you are going down Penobscot, just like we, and you see a canoe come out of bank and go along before you, but you no see 'em stream. That is *Sunkhaze*."

He had previously complimented me on my paddling, saying that I paddled "just like anybody," giving me an

Indian name which meant "great paddler." When off this stream he said to me, who sat in the bows, "Me teach you paddle."

So, turning toward the shore, he got out, came forward, and placed my hands as he wished. He placed one of them quite outside the boat, and the other parallel with the first, grasping the paddle near the end, not over the flat extremity, and told me to slide it back and forth on the side of the canoe. This, I found, was a great improvement which I had not thought of, saving me the labor of lifting the paddle each time, and I wondered that he had not suggested it before. It is true, before our baggage was reduced we had been obliged to sit with our legs drawn up, and our knees above the side of the canoe, which would have prevented our paddling thus, or perhaps he was afraid of wearing out his canoe by constant friction on the side.

I told him that I had been accustomed to sit in the stern, and lift my paddle at each stroke, getting a pry on the side each time, and I still paddled partly as if in the stern. He then wanted to see me paddle in the stern. So, changing paddles, for he had the longer and better one, and turning end for end, he sitting flat on the bottom and I on the crossbar, he began to paddle very hard, trying to turn the canoe, looking over his shoulder and laughing, but, finding it in vain, he relaxed his efforts, though we still sped along a mile or two very swiftly. He said that he had no fault to find with my paddling in the stern, but I complained that he did not paddle according to his own directions in the bows.

As we drew near to Oldtown I asked Polis if he was not glad to get home again; but there was no relenting to his wildness, and he said, "It makes no difference to me where I am." Such is the Indian's pretense always.

We approached the Indian Island through the narrow strait called "Cook." He said: "I 'xpect we take in some water there, river so high—never see it so high at this season. Very rough water there; swamp steamboat once. Don't you paddle till I tell you. Then you paddle right along."

It was a very short rapid. When we were in the midst of it he shouted, "Paddle!" and we shot through without taking in a drop. Soon after the Indian houses came in sight. I could not at first tell my companion which of two or three large white ones was our guide's. He said it was the one with blinds.

We landed opposite his door at about four in the afternoon, having come some forty miles this day. We stopped for an hour at his house. Mrs. P. wore a hat and had a silver brooch on her breast, but she was not introduced to us. The house was roomy and neat. A large new map of Oldtown and the Indian Island hung on the wall, and a clock opposite to it.

This was the last that I saw of Joe Polis. We took the last train, and reached Bangor that night.